FRONTIER ELEMENTS

IN A

HUDSON RIVER VILLAGE

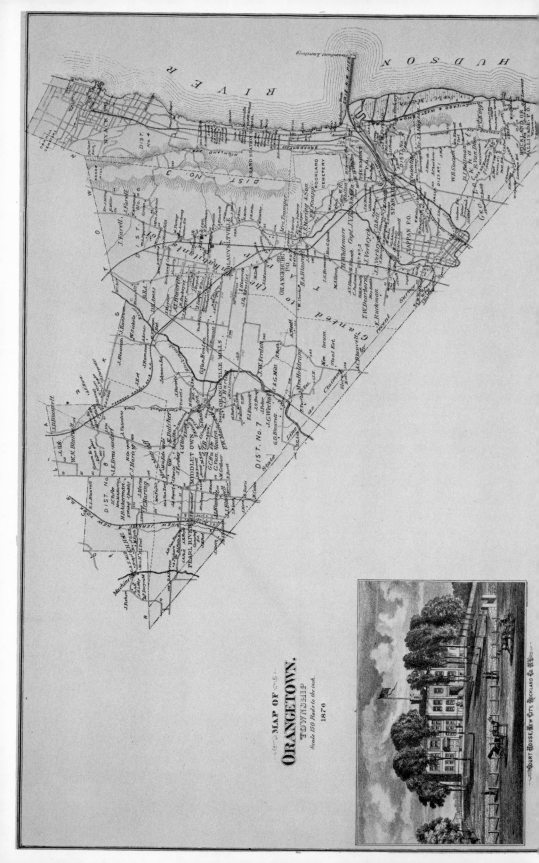

MAP OF
ORANGETOWN.
TOWNSHIP
Scale 150 Rods to the inch.
1876

- COURT HOUSE, NEW CITY, ROCKLAND CO. N.Y. -

CARL NORDSTROM

FRONTIER ELEMENTS

IN A

HUDSON RIVER VILLAGE

NATIONAL UNIVERSITY PUBLICATIONS
KENNIKAT PRESS • 1973
PORT WASHINGTON, N.Y. • LONDON

KENNIKAT PRESS

NATIONAL UNIVERSITY PUBLICATIONS

SERIES IN AMERICAN STUDIES

General Editor

JAMES P. SHENTON

Professor of History, Columbia University

Library of Congress Catalog Card No.: 72-91175
ISBN: 0-8046-9033-2

Manufactured in the United States of America

Published by
Kennikat Press, Inc.
Port Washington, N.Y./London

PREFACE

In this work a theory about people in the United States is tested through a close study of economic and social relations in a New York State community. The theory, the frontier thesis of Frederick Jackson Turner and others, is first developed as an ideal type and then subjected to examination in terms delineated by experience in a place of limited size. That place is the village of Nyack, New York, and the surrounding area. Activities there are followed closely and investigated in concrete detail. It is hoped that through this close attention, understanding and identification will become possible for the reader.

If this identification has in any sense been achieved, two persons, long since dead, deserve special recognition because their work was essential to it. They are Dr. Frank B. Green, who devoted his short but productive life to the illumination of Nyack's history, and George H. Budke who, during the early years of this century, collected and annotated a great mass of historical material relevant to the community.

Among the many whose assistance was invaluable during the research phase of this study, I am especially indebted to the staff of the Nyack library for their interest, cooperation, and unfailing enthusiasm. They have always made their library a friendly place.

During work on an earlier version of the book, I received help and encouragement from Professors Felicia Deyrup, Arvid Brodersen, and Adolph Lowe of the New School for Social Research. I am also indebted to Stephen Fay for his incisive comments and to Robert Leydenfrost for his assistance with the maps.

Finally, my heartfelt thanks to Ms. Holly Henderson for her gracious assistance in preparing the manuscript for publication.

CARL NORDSTROM

South Nyack, New York

CONTENTS

MAPS

TABLES

FRONTIER ELEMENTS

IN A

HUDSON RIVER VILLAGE

1

NEWS FROM ORANGE COUNTY

News of an event unique in the annals of universal history had begun to circulate in the Western world as early as the eighteenth century. According to information then current in Europe, a human metamorphosis of profound implications had occurred on the sea-coast and in the forests of the New World. A new mode of living, founded on equality and reason, had been established there, and for once it seemed that effort and industry, rather than position and birth, would finally be rewarded. With the passage across the sea, it was said, the chains forged of ancient tradition were being discarded and people found themselves free to express their natural vigor and compassion.

Writing from his farm in Orange County, New York, Hector St. John de Crèvecœur first proclaimed the fabulous news in 1782. In his *Letters from an American Farmer* he asserted that the individuals of many nations had been melted together into a new race in America. The prejudices and manners of their former existence had evaporated. New attitudes and modes of action appropriate to American circumstances had replaced them, dominant among which was a respect for self–interest. This was, in his opinion, what nature had intended; that labor should receive its just reward. No longer was the better part of its product to be claimed by the despot, the rich abbot, or the mighty lord. In the fullness of his optimism

3

de Crèvecœur then asked, what was this American, this product of liberation, "this new man?"

Throughout the following century many others carried the glad tidings back to Europe.[1] Again and again they proclaimed the fresh and exciting news. Most important among these harbingers was another author of French descent, Alexis de Tocqueville. He had travelled extensively throughout the United States early in the 1830s, collecting information on prisons and penitentiaries for his government. On his return to France and following completion of his official report on the trip, he wrote *Democracy in America,* in which he summarized his general observations about life on the new continent. Comprehensive in its scope and classic in its confidence, it was also notable for its intelligence, precision, and thoroughness.

Democracy as a distinctive form of human interaction was the central theme of de Tocqueville's study. To him, it seemed destined to dominate Europe in the immediate future. He believed that a great revolution was in process throughout the Old World and that this revolution was sure to succeed. The removal of privilege and the leveling of men to equality one to another would be a product of this new democracy. Embracing the revolution as inevitable, de Tocqueville then argued that it was important for responsible men to examine those ways of life which were already founded on democratic principles. It seemed to him that the United States provided an opportunity for just such an examination.

Democracy in America begins by discussing the novelty to the European eye of commonplace experiences in the United States and underscores the impact equality in social relationships seems to have had on those experiences. In de Tocqueville's formulation, progress towards a generalized interpersonal equality and towards its political form—democracy—was already far advanced here. He felt that two circumstances accounted for this: one referred primarily to social class, and the second was more precisely economic. First, he argued, the settlers in America generally had been individual human products of poverty and misfortune in the Old World and, consequently, had had no concept of any superiority of some of their number over others when they crossed the ocean. In effect, they had been delivered on the colonial shores innocent of prerogatives founded

---

1. Cf. Commager, *America in Perspective,* a compendium of excerpts from such reports, for a more complete understanding of their general tone and variety.

on rank and privilege. In the second place, according to de Tocqueville, economic practices in the New World had not provided a suitable base for the development of class distinctions. Conditions here, he maintained, obliged landlords—*even* landlords, that is—to toil in the fields alongside their hired hands. As a result no aristocracy had been able to develop. Given these special circumstances, he concluded, interpersonal equality had had a unique opportunity to flourish in the former British colonies.

While de Tocqueville acknowledged the importance of cultural patterns transplanted from the old country, he asserted that the germ of egalitarian democracy was to be found in all colonies, whether French, Spanish, or English. Certain special circumstances, however, had encouraged its flourishing in the United States, which, in his opinion, made it the proper place to examine the new universal form of society then materializing throughout the world.

The singular social environment of the United States continued to evoke the interest of foreign journalists, travellers, and men of affairs during the remainder of the nineteenth century. Struck by the energy, sentimentality, pragmatism, and vulgarity they found everywhere present here, they elaborated at length on the characteristics of this unique experience, the lessons it might contain, and the people themselves.

To native American observers, the national experience was also of great interest, but their emphasis was somewhat different. True to their booster spirit, they more often celebrated the superiority of the nation's institutions rather than the uniqueness of its people. This difference in emphasis had a predictably useful purpose for an eminently practical people—to educate the young and prepare them for their eventual political task. If the government erected of, by, and for the people was to function properly, certain faith in its structures was needed. In its schools America's political institutions were promoted as having the nature of fundamental truth, and thus the necessary faith was inculcated.

In their scholarly papers and in the school texts they prepared from those papers, America's savants described these institutions as the end product of five millennia of evolution in the development of human political intelligence. Continuity of mores and customs was a prime focus of their work. Yet also a difference was claimed: it was argued that in the journey across the sea, these same mores and customs had somehow been improved and purified. America, its chroniclers asserted, had provided a unique opportunity to select the good and reject the bad, to the benefit of the world at large. Possibly some essential need to maintain the illusion of roots in the Old World conditioned their approach. In any case, American scholars emphasized the way people had arranged their relationships in the United States, and less so the singularity of experience here. In their opinion America offered a better way of life because it had been designed to the specifications of a practical people who had been more wise rather than merely different. As a result more than a century was to elapse before de Crèvecœur's putative new man and his unique environment would be closely studied by native American scholars.

The occasion for the formulation of these various observations, both foreign and native, into a comprehensive thesis embodying interesting ideological implications was the annual meeting of the American Historical Association in 1893. At that meeting a young Wisconsin professor, Frederick Jackson Turner, called attention to the announcement by the Superintendent of the Census in 1890 of the closing of the United States frontier. Turner then went on to argue, in contradistinction to opinion current among historians of the time, that the explanation for the peculiar nature of American institutions was to be found at the scene of the action itself, in the New World. These institutions, he declared, had been compelled to adapt themselves to the requirements of an expanding people, "to the changes involved in crossing a continent, in winning a wilderness . . ."[2] To the influence of the frontier, the outer edge of settlement, he attributed the development of unique social and economic institutions and, further, of a composite nationality for the American people.

With Turner's paper the tidings de Tocqueville and his contemporaries had carried from the New World to the Old had returned to their source. Turner's influence waxed vigorous during the early third of the new century, and important people regarded him highly. It is claimed his evangel even reached the White House. The doctrine's appeal, no doubt, as much mythological as scientific, encouraged a national identity, established cultural autonomy for

2. Turner, *Frontier*, p. 2.

the United States, emphasized that virtue was implicit in people conditioned by frontier experience, and underscored what was seen as the superiority of the American way of life.

The historical moment was also right. With the Old World losing its grip a new leadership was clearly needed; who was better fitted to serve than the son of the frontier? In Turner's formulation, it was readily apparent that through the raw experience of frontier living the contaminations of the past had been eradicated and the natural good in mankind had been released. Conceived in purity, nourished on liberty and its concomitant equality, and secure in his confidence, this "new man" was uncommonly well prepared to assume his rightful place on the world stage—or so it seemed. And his opportunity was not long in coming. It was only a few years after Turner had enunciated the frontier doctrine that the "new man" embraced his appointed task and marched off to save the world for democracy and to bring to all mankind a better way of life.

The Turner thesis also had its scientific appeal. Through its mediation historians were liberated from an arid concern about European origins and were emboldened to develop an empirical approach to their subject instead. Many welcomed this opportunity; empiricism suited the American taste. With Turner, who remained active in the further development of the thesis, they worked at extending its relevance, scope, and application.[3] By the close of the 1920s, according to R. A. Billington, the frontier thesis reigned supreme in American historiography. Its uncontested reign was of short duration, however, for with the advent of the depression reaction set in. During the darker days of that troubled time a vigorous criticism of Turner and his supporters developed, which reaction still continues to erupt on occasion. More recently, a critical examination of the thesis informed by conceptual systems developed within the disciplines of economics, sociology, and anthropology has been under way.[4]

Today the frontier thesis seems best understood as a comprehensive product combining Turner's original formulation with the works of his supporters, as well as of those who joined in the critical

3. Cf. Billington, *America's Frontier Heritage*, pp. 288-291, for a bibliography relevant to this development.
4. Cf. Hofstadter and Lipset, *Turner and the Frontier Sociology*, a set of essays centered on this contemporary examination.

attack during the thirties and of those who seek to re-evaluate the thesis in terms of other disciplines. In complex combination these various claims and challenges constitute a thesis which in its totality stands as the most comprehensive statement extant which seeks to explain the origins of an American way of life and of the logic implicit in its folkways and customs.

A precise interpretation of intended meanings in Turner's text itself is difficult since his offerings are both eclectic and cluttered—a hodgepodge of grand inspirations, penetrating observations, and obsolete ideas. They are of a piece with the American society they seek to define. Within them, however, two contrasting frames of reference predominate. One, which is conceptually dynamic, sees the frontier as a phase in evolution, or as a passing moment in the grand march from primitive savagery to the advanced civilization of great cities. In this frame of reference the approach attributed earlier to the American savants can be discerned. The second sees the frontier as a fixed illusion about an ongoing present and can be formulated as a paradigm composed of institutions and modes of action adapted to frontier living. Here we return to ground explored by de Crèvecœur, for the one who does the adapting and composing would be his "new man." To Turner, this paradigm has played a significant role in defining the content of American culture. Taken together they introduce an element of ambiguity into the thesis itself and account for much of the critical challenge Turner's work has inspired.[5]

Nevertheless, Turner's thesis is not essentially contradictory and the ambiguity implied is textual rather than fundamental. Utilizing approaches suggested by the body of criticism which emphasizes the social science disciplines, the thesis can be restated provisionally in terms that include both contrasting frames of reference. Following Turner, we can maintain that frontier conditions in the United States promoted in the pioneers the development of a set of personal and social characteristics typified by self–reliance, interpersonal equality, and independence. Exemplified by typical economic, political, and social manifestations as institutions, these characteristics form a unique social configuration associated with life on the frontier. Turner has apparently derived this configuration from direct observations and his extensive acquaintance with the literature of life at the frontier.

5. Turner, *op. cit.*, p. 22. Cf. Billington, *op. cit.*, Chapter 3, p. 25, 39, and pp. 47-68.

Furthermore, Turner implies, short–run social forces, themselves the product of frontier experience, will maintain the stability of this configuration even after the frontier has moved west. And finally, he suggests that when the frontier configuration is inconsistent with the needs of the post–frontier areas, long–run social forces operate to break it down and replace it with one more suitable to the objective situation. Given a formulation along these lines, evidence of the retention of a frontier way of thinking and acting after the frontier itself had drifted west would not necessarily negate a long–run shift away from such behavior and towards a pattern of culture similar to that of the European fatherland. Such a formulation of Turner's ideas is, of course, highly abstract and misses much of the vigorous flavor of his interpretation of frontier life. Hence it is deficient, albeit useful.

Throughout the study that follows we have sought to utilize the heuristic properties of the received frontier thesis in closely examining a segment of American experience. In that sense it represents a continuation of work already done, especially during the latest period when efforts to develop a sociology of the frontier, an anthropology of the frontier, and an economy of the frontier have been under way. To facilitate technical comprehension an ideal–type model of the frontier is offered in the next chapter. This model has been constructed out of material mined from Turner's work as well as from that of his advocates and critics.

The area chosen for scrutiny is a place of modest size and is offered as a microcosm which allows for close observation of the activities of specific individuals as they go about their daily living. Given the limitations of public records, we want to get to know our subjects as well as we can, to try to gain some understanding of their outlook—some *verstehen,* in the sense Max Weber uses that term—and, also, to avoid treating them simply as frozen artifacts of an abstract principle about the frontier and its impact. In effect, we mean to follow our people about, to look over their shoulders, to become acquainted with their associates, and by means of this gossip's approach, to experience with them their problems and their moments of joy. In making this effort we have been guided by certain recent work in philosophy and social science which seeks to elucidate dynamic elements in interpersonal activities through adherence to a dialectical approach.[6]

In the interest of intelligibility we have concentrated throughout on specific individuals and families. Altogether, the life histories of some two thousand individuals were reconstructed—to the degree possible using publicly available sources—for this study. Extensive use was made of obituaries, census tracts, and items from newspapers. Only a few of these people can be introduced to the reader, who would otherwise be overwhelmed by innumerable names and life stories. The individuals introduced are offered as representative and are not necessarily those whose achievements reflect the greatest credit on the community.

Such a method excludes many who, with other information, would be worthy of study. Most often, and most unfortunately, it excludes females, since during the period studied their activities were largely confined to the family. Wherever possible the same individuals reappear in subsequent incidents. To have presented them thus does not mean that those whose activities are emphasized are the only or even the most prominent individuals participating in the various events. In the main they are those whose activities are most all–inclusive. It is our intention that those chosen as representatives be allowed to retain the fullness of their humanity. A close study incorporating the frontier thesis should not reduce its people to the role of pawns to the principle. Concentrating on their work and their play in a setting defined by their needs and ambitions, we have attempted to understand and describe the encounters of de Crèvecœur's "new man" as he grew older.

We see the Turner approach in its largest sense as eminently dialectical, as a way of describing the praxis of people who find they must come to grips with a necessity growing out of material experience. They both cope with that experience, with greater or lesser efficiency, and talk about what it has meant to them. Through concrete acts, and in the search for meaning, they affect transformations in the fabric of their experience. Thus, throughout, our study is concerned primarily with events and subsequent transformations in an American locality as they are illuminated by the frontier thesis and only incidentally with an abstract set of definitions referring to that thesis. Envisioning a process in which pure frontier praxis may have

---

6. Cf. Sartre, *Problem of Method,* and Laing and Cooper, *Reason and Violence, passim,* also Vidich and Bensman, *Small Town and Mass Society,* especially for chapters on methodology in the second edition, pp. 317-475.

existed "momentarily" as a synthetic product of coping with existence on the open land of North America, we are interested in events following the putative period of the frontier as well as those accompanying the "moment" itself.

In the main body of this work the model of the frontier way of life which we will introduce in the next chapter will be used to regulate the examination of the chosen microcosm. Keep in mind, however, that the fundamental emphasis should always be on the relationships of individual men and women in their world, on the limits necessity imposes on them, and on their signifying acts. It should not be on the abstracting and reducing capacities of the thesis. The effort should be towards capturing and, if possible, experiencing the quality of the dialectical process as it unfolds.

It is important to situate our microcosm with precision, geographically, to know what it means when an individual says he has spent the day in a nearby town, or why a group of individuals settles in a certain spot. With our interest centered on dialectical transformations, it is also necessary to choose a location which has been settled for a period sufficient to allow for the occurrence of a succession of complex events—a location in which, as we said earlier, the "new man" has had an opportunity to grow older. The area chosen for study is in the East. Although Turner gave only spotty attention to eastern events in his work, the East, too, was once frontier. It also satisfies our time criterion because by the mid–nineteenth century observers no longer seemed to consider it a frontier area.

The locality we have chosen to study carries with it a special bonus, for it is near the place where de Crèvecœur wrote his letters. In fact, during the colonial period when de Crèvecœur was actually farming and writing, the area we plan to examine was legally a part of the same Orange County from which de Crèvecœur proclaimed his fabulous news.

The locus of our study will be Nyack, New York, and its immediate vicinity. Nyack is a small city on the Hudson River in what is now Rockland County. Structurally it is a trinity—a series of three incorporated villages comprising a single economic unit. These three consubstantial villages are named Upper Nyack, Nyack, and South Nyack. They lie on a plateau bounded by the river on one side and the hills bordering the river on the other. They are approximately twenty miles north of New York City.

Depending on the nature of specific events under consideration, the boundaries of what we mean by "the vicinity of Nyack" will vary from time to time. For some occasions, the horizon of society will be drawn narrowly around the villages, but for others it will extend to the boundaries of the county. Early in the history of this area Nyack is not sharply differentiated from the township in which it is located (Orangetown) or the county (at first, Orange, and after the Revolutionary War, Rockland). Later events, however, come to center in the three villages. To the degree possible we shall allow the events themselves to define the geographic range and extent of significient social interaction. Most properly, Nyack should be understood as a prime locus of intermingled interactions, a nexus of social relations, rather than as a separate and distinct category of interaction.

This work will be an argument from the particular and, as such, can be expected to suffer all the weaknesses with which such an argument is likely to be burdened. We cannot achieve our purpose unless we stay close to the people we are studying. It is necessary for us to live with them through their particular experiences as intensively as possible. By this means we hope to discover their intentions for ourselves.

2
A PLACE WHERE FREEDOM CAN WORK

In this chapter we offer a construct of the frontier as an ideal–type configuration, delineating specific frontier characteristics taken from Turner and others. Throughout the remainder of the work this configuration will serve as a guide for examining experience in Nyack and vicinity. With the aid of this operational definition of the frontier situation, we should be able to ascertain the extent to which Nyack experience reflected frontier activity and, further, the extent to which concrete action there initiated its own transformations and revealed unexamined possibilities.

The configuration utilized has been distilled from the many comments Turner, his supporters, and his critics have published about frontier activities and frontier people. It is not meant to be original. Furthermore, the word "alleged" or some similar synonym belongs with almost every statement offered, for often these are only claimed characteristics and have not been verified through systematic research. The configuration also should not be taken as universal in application. The descriptive statements on which it is founded are only those reported about the frontier in the United States and ignore similar experience elsewhere.[1] They are the perti-

---

1. Marvin Mikesell, for one, criticizes Turner and his followers for their neglect of comparative research. Cf. Mikesell, "Comparative Studies in Frontier History," in Hofstadter and Lipset, *Turner and the Frontier Sociology,* pp. 152-71.

nent ones, however; they form the explicit basis for the frontier thesis as it is conventionally understood in American social science.

To Turner and his closest supporters, the frontier was first open land, an edge of nothingness where people from Europe and from the eastern seaboard of America could move at will. The word frontier, as he used it, also suggests a special relationship between such people and that land. In most accounts the Indian, who had previously lived there, is forgotten. Either he has already left the stage to others, or, where he has remained, he is seen solely as an inconvenience to progress. Conventionally, this land seems to have been thought of as empty space, to be exploited at the pleasure of newcomers to the area. While several authors speak of the town as the second stage of the frontier,[2] the orthodox approach to frontier memorabilia focuses on the land itself and, more precisely, on land utilized for agriculture.

Although Turner and others use the term "free land" in describing the frontier, the important factor in the relationship between the new people and the open land was not so much the low cost of the land as its relative abundance. To Turner, the frontier was held to be a land of opportunity and freedom and, given that claim, isolation and spatial distance were of great importance as determinants. Paxon, for one, in his definitive article on the frontier in the *Encyclopaedia of the Social Sciences,* emphasizes the role social distance played in fostering frontier attributes in persons. Following a convention set by the Census Bureau and emphasizing the essential social distance, he defines the agrarian frontier as an area with from two to six inhabitants per square mile—in other words, an area in which family households were located on farms situated about a mile apart. This low population density is to him the significant frontier agent because it enforces isolation and preserves social distance.

Of course, demography alone did not define the agrarian frontier. Had conditions warranted, people might still have crowded together, no matter how abundant the space. To effect its unique impact the Turner frontier required a special technical pattern of

2. For example, Elkins and McKitrick identify two levels of frontier experience; one is called primitive or agrarian, and a second is characterized by town life. See "A Meaning for Turner's Frontier," *Political Science Quarterly,* LXIX (September, 1954), pp. 339-41.

land tenure, one operating so as to sustain the necessary isolation and social distance. Small farms, held in fee simple and worked by resident householders, farms which could be operated, in the main, as single, self–sufficient household units, define the correct technical pattern. Such farms should be compact, relatively equal in size, and distributed evenly throughout the countryside. Also, while these farms need not be free to the new settler, their price should be well within the means of the ordinary operator. In *The Making of an American Community* Merle Curti points out that in Trempealeau County, Wisconsin, a reasonable mortgage arrangement played an important role in enabling people to acquire farms and make them productive. Finally, the prevailing legal system should be such as to ensure absolute proprietary rights for the independent operators. In short, neither plantations nor manors had a place on Turner's frontier.

A low population density and a suitable tenure arrangement, while necessary elements in defining a frontier situation, are not alone sufficient. Abundance is not simply a matter of space; the land must be workable and fruitful, as well. Potter, in *People of Plenty*, identifies fertility and productivity as central to the understanding of the American character. He then singles out the frontier as a context in which abundance occurred. While his interpretation takes us well beyond the frontier itself, it does point to an important building block in the frontier thesis. Assuredly, for the agrarian frontier to be viable, it was essential that the land provide the wherewithal for prosperity.

Several authors in their descriptions of prevailing living conditions on the frontier have emphasized the self–sufficiency of the frontier people.[3] Others have pointed to their primary concern with the material aspects of living and claimed that little time was left for idle speculation and self–indulgence.[4] Such observations underline another important feature of the typical frontier. Generally, the economic activities of the pioneers are conditioned by need rather than by competence, and ingenuity—the ability to get along with a simple technology and to improvise, if necessary—is held

---

3. For example, Rupert B. Vance, "Frontier—Geographical and Social Aspects," *Encyclopaedia of the Social Sciences*, VI, p. 503; also Craven, *Democracy*, p. 48.
4. John D. Hicks, "The Development of Civilization in the Middle West," in Fox, *Culture in the Middle West*, p. 79, and Burkhart, "The Turner Thesis," *Wisconsin History*, XXXI (1947-48), p. 74.

to be more significant for survival than are equipment and skill. In this aspect the frontiersman is envisioned as an independent, non-specialized producer, who is usually a jack–of–all–trades and, above all, resourceful.

On the typical frontier the land must be fruitful and the technology to work it well within the capacities of the ordinary farm operator. As a result, dependence on one's fellow farmers is minimized and a superstructure of supply houses and repair shops is not needed. The pioneers are thereby enabled to settle at a distance from each other as well as from servicing centers. In consequence, the spatial isolation essential to Paxson's formulation of the frontier thesis becomes possible. If, then, no special need for protection exists, the frontier family is able to provide for itself and operate as an isolated unit.

Thus abundance, an appropriate tenure system, and a simple productive technique allowed the development of a total economic system which can be described as atomic and potentially liberating. A nineteenth–century concept of "atomic" is intended, of course; one in which independent entities—the isolated, largely self–sufficient farm households—exist in relative indifference to each other. The situation is seen to be liberating in the sense that, within limits, social relationships are untrammeled. The individuals—here, households—are free to combine with others into social groups or to scorn at will.

The atomized social structure carries with it certain political and cultural corollaries. For one, the same distance that encourages self–sufficiency also situates the several farmers beyond the reach of organizing authority. Given a clear title to their land, some access to markets, and security from marauders, these pioneers have little need for the good offices of government. Thanks to self–sufficiency, they are also not especially vulnerable to administrative coercion. Of course, a willful man carrying a gun is a threat and requires suppression should he insist on disrupting peace, but such concerns, while exciting, were largely incidental on the frontier. The normal course of affairs minimized opportunities for the exercise of power.

With interdependence among the frontier settlers theoretically a matter of little importance, the disciplining force it imposes in most social situations was largely absent. Nevertheless, everyone who had settled on the frontier was in some sense the product of a traditional way of life, and it is reported that individuals sharing a common tradition often located on contiguous farms. In fact, Curti, in stressing Norwegians, Vermonters, and other such tribal categories throughout *The Making of an American Community,* suggests that these ethnic and locational identities were an important fact of frontier existence and that contiguous settlement of like peoples was the common practice. Assistance from one's ethnic fellows was certainly a positive asset for the pioneer seeking to get a farm established. Thus, traditional systems did persist in the new world and frequently were important in a supportive sense. They lacked binding force, however, for the farmer was not dependent on their good offices for his livelihood. While he may have needed help in getting established, he did not necessarily need that same help on a continuing basis. The material situation epitomizing the frontier favored his making it on his own—and rewarded him for doing so.

Had the pioneers settled together in a tight group and/or under the control of some instituted authority, it is probable that they would have retained a more substantially tradition–directed orientation. But, if we are to accept conventional assertions about frontier life, they did not. Instead, they located their homesteads at a distance from each other and, unconstrained by the bondage of the past, they sought their private advantage in competition with their fellows. Thanks to their isolation and their self–sufficiency they could afford not to be submissive; indeed, they could afford to be obstinate in the presence of those whom former tradition had taught them to respect.

In sum, then, the atomized society of the agrarian frontier separates one from those potentially in authority, permits an egalitarian disposition in relation to others, and provides many opportunities for the expression of independence. As a result a sense of freedom from custom's bonds is encouraged.

Frontierspeople, the human product of this liberating experience, had special characteristics, Turner claimed. This emphasis of his led Pierson to describe the frontier thesis, in part, as "a sort of social psychology."[5] According to Turner, individualism and an exuberant spirit dominate the make–up of the frontiersman. In

5. Pierson, "Frontier and American Institutions," *New England Quarterly,* XV (1942), p. 230.

another context he spoke of the pioneer's "restless energy, . . . quick capacity for judgment and action, . . . belief in liberty." He described them as emotional, having faith in themselves and their destiny, and speculated that perhaps, because "of the usual isolation of their lives, when they came together in associations whether of the camp meeting or the political gathering, they felt the influence of a common emotion and enthusiasm."[6]

For Turner, then, frontier circumstances fashioned people who were accustomed to operate in an uncharted environment, who were sure of their personal capacity to remedy confusion and certain of their future prosperity, and who were enamored with the idea of improvement. It rewarded those who functioned well where disorder prevailed, and thereby promoted rugged individualism. It also —and this he did not emphasize—buried those who were unable to survive in the demanding environment.

For this romance also had its darker side. There exists a body of testimony which stands in direct contrast to Turner's euphoria. It is frequently offered by historians considered to be supporters of Turner. Paxson, for one, suggests that the frontier induced homogeneity in its population through "a sort of inverted democractization that worked by leveling the exceptional man down rather than by lifting the common man up."[7] Craven also stresses a similar point, arguing that the stern necessities of the simple life demanded conformity in conduct, "so that each man might know what to expect of the other."[8] Accordingly, people were pounded into a common pattern. There was little place for dreamers on the frontier, he continued, as men must turn to present tasks, to tilling the soil, to riding the fences, to killing the predators, if they were to survive.

We have then two sets of testimony, two psychological patterns standing in contrast to each other, one extolling the pioneer for his independence and individualism, and a second emphasizing conformity. For an explanation of the paradox let us turn again to the frontier itself.

As has been indicated, each household was relatively self—sufficient, isolated, and inhabited by people who were, ostensibly, recent arrivals. Functionally, each of these independent households

6. Turner, *Frontier*, pp. 37, 263, 345.
7. Paxson, *Great Demobilization*, p. 37.
8. Craven, *Democracy*, p. 47.

was its own base of power—that is the meaning of the claimed independence. This power had its limits, however. Within a certain narrow scope of action the separate householders were autonomous and could do what they thought they should. Their land was their own, to use as they saw fit. All that was required of them was that they produce goods in sufficient quantity to survive. Their children, their attitudes and beliefs, and their aspirations were their own business and no one else's. Or, at least, that is the way it was supposed to be.

Peace was primarily what the householders required of their neighbors—to be left alone. When it prevailed, the cherished autonomy could be sustained. Of course, conflicts might arise, for these neighbors were also strangers; in the case of such conflicts, equal rights before the law were mandatory. This doctrine of equality, combined with a firm defense of property rights—another form of the same doctrine—provided for the maintenance of household independence. The other surrounding households deserved neither more nor less.

That the separate householders were nominally strangers, each to the other, is what was important. The technical significance of settling as an immigrant in a new land lay in this strangeness and in the distrust it inspired. As strangers by definition, the pioneers must always have been unsure in their interpersonal dealings. With strangeness ubiquitous, responses founded on conventional expectations about the acts of others were likely to go awry. In the move to the frontier the cake of custom had been broken. It had to be mixed and leavened and baked anew with each additional social relationship undertaken.

The men and women of the frontier were not simply strangers, they might also be enemies. Competitors in a marketplace economy, their personal advantage was often founded on the failure or ineptness of another nearby. When competition was intense, when one's neighbors spoke a different language or performed odd ceremonies —and frontier circumstances were frequently so—each recognized that he must walk carefully in the presence of his fellows for fear that he might inspire some negativity on the other's part towards himself. Consequently, the social order on the atomized frontier was, at best, precarious.

Both daring and caution were of service. With communication

among the independent strangers difficult to arrange and often awkward, the frontiersman resorted to bravado. This bravado was what Turner took for restless energy and enthusiasm. Inventions, new techniques, and projects designed to meet immediate needs returned direct benefits, and were readily admired by the practical–minded pioneers. The easygoing fellow who could break the ice with a song or story made the social occasion more pleasant. And fierce advocacy in politics, centered on issues of minor significance, provided an opportunity for communication. When contained within reasonable boundaries such bravado, invention, and sociability served to break down isolation and became a conventional form of deportment for the multitude of strangers.

The range within which such independence was allowed its head was strictly limited, nevertheless. Any claim for special treatment had to be denied for it constituted a threat to the balanced order. As status and prestige, implied or assumed, both carry power, they were emphatically rejected. Extant, they provided fuel for the endemic distrust. When recognized, such as in the form of superior education or fancy ways, they were to be condemned or, at least, their carriers were. Seeking self–protection, the separate households of strangers joined together to counteract those who stood outside and were secure in their indifference. This wariness towards the exceptional individual was the source of much frontier conformity and also of its anti-intellectualism. To the frontier person the average, plus a mild standard of deviation, was all that could be endured.

The paradox implicit in this "sort of social psychology" helps explain the contradictory element in the various treatments of the frontier as a melting pot. We have already noted that the pioneers were nominally free of traditional ties and that their material situation favored independent action. In theory, they could ignore their neighbors and still survive with some degree of comfort. Turner and others, in keeping with this inference, stressed the plastic and absorptive characteristics of frontier experience and emphasized that "in the crucible of the frontier the immigrants were Americanized, liberated, and fused into a mixed race."[9] In this manner they underscored the alienating elements of frontier experience and accentuated the transforming impact of a situation fostering self–sufficiency.

9. Turner, *op. cit.*, p. 23. Cf. Burkhart, *op. cit.*, p. 72, and Paxson, *loc. cit.*, *Encyclopaedia of the Social Sciences*, VI, p. 501.

On the other hand, careful studies of frontier experience, such as Curti's detailed examination of Trempealeau County in Wisconsin, and Vogt's ethnographic report on Homestead, New Mexico, refer to the persistence of tradition–defining traits in frontier–type situations. To a certain extent the pioneer experience seems to have encouraged the retention of ethnic sentiments, but at a cost. The foreigner whose strangeness was built in stood in danger of being singled out as threatening, as was anyone who was exceptional. Formally, the frontier people were strangers to each other, and had to learn to cope with that estrangement. Some who found the alienation oppressive sought the closeness of their kind, placing their dependence on tribal relationships carried over from prior situations. Others, able to function comfortably within the alienating environment, reaped advantage from their freedom. They still may have longed, however, for some secure base on which to found their claims for respect—a longing which may explain the appeal of patriotism in frontier communities.

At this point we cannot pursue who the "some" and the "others" were or why. Still, what we can say is that at the typical frontier one would expect to find in some persons the persistence of prior cultural experience reflected in their social relationships and activities, and in others a considerable indifference to folkways from the past. One group would identify with the Old World, the other with the New World, and to the extent that an individual carried both tendencies within himself, he would be subject to a personal tension of greater or less severity.

Up to this point we have stressed the atomic structure of frontier society and have emphasized the extent to which it was founded on a material situation in which self–sufficiency was archetypical. In so reifying frontier experience, however, we have slighted occasions where the cooperation of one's neighbors was highly desirable. It is time that we removed the artificial brackets which have allowed us to concentrate on the implications of atomized frontier existence and give our attention to such occasions of cooperation and the imperatives which they in turn established.

In general, before the soil could be used for productive purposes, an intensive investment in land improvement was necessary. The householder had to spend much time in clearing, in construction, in well–digging, and road–building for access. Such complex operations often involved the specialized skills of one's neighbors as well as their cooperation. To raise a barn or to build a bridge would call for shared activity by several individuals working in close conjunction. Harvest, also, provided many opportunities for collective activity, and the husking bee, for example, has become prototypical of country life in America. Surveying and the locating of sites for wells required the skills of specialists as did marriages and christenings. There were, in other words, many occasions for individuals to work together to their mutual advantage.

There was also the sticky business of regulating relationships among the purported equals so that conflicts would be discouraged and discord minimized. Records had to be maintained, clashes among close neighbors mediated, and contractual agreements enforced. Above all, the public peace must be preserved, and government in some form, even at the frontier, was required. Preferably, such government as there was should be that government which governs least, but none the less it was government.

The frontiersman handled collective enterprise in a characteristic way. Typically independent and self–reliant, he placed a price on his willingness to share. He looked to his own private advantage. As a result, the only means by which unity of action could be arranged at the frontier was through public agreements in which the demands of those planning to participate in a common action were clearly specified. Such agreements were contractual rather than conventional and commonly included among their provisions precise boundaries to the actions possible under their authorization. These legal prescriptions were designed to protect essentially private associators from domination by the collective other. It was this cooperating individualism, specifying rights and including both stated ends and stated sanctions, which made collective social action possible for the free people of the frontier.

Collective action at the frontier was thus an arrangement among equals. Often spontaneous and originating in simple, informal contacts, such arrangements frequently developed into complex associations which were carefully designed to exploit an opportunity or to fill a need. Turner describes such associations as having been "extemporized by voluntary action," and lays emphasis on their lack of formal connection with immemorial custom or governmental compulsion. Intended for the performance of specific tasks, they were organized into whatever order their designers deemed appropriate. Such associations were public, limited in scope, and, generally, hedged with qualifications. In summing up his understanding of Turner's conception of frontier society, Pierson declared that it had ". . . four parts and only four: government, business, education, and religion. And the essence of these was freedom."[10]

In government the emphasis was on free institutions, for democratic–type techniques of organization were held to be especially fitted to the situation. Governments organized along democratic lines were deemed to be legitimate, because they alone operated to protect the individual's inalienable right to function as he saw fit. However, the officials of such governments, whether elected or appointed, were automatically distrusted, and a system of checks and balances was included in the carefully drawn contractual documents upon which the government was founded. The provisions for the setting of ground rules, through which the voluntary associations were enabled to perform necessary tasks requiring organized effort, were especially important. With the members of the general public largely independent and possibly willful, such ground rules were essential if anything was to be accomplished.

Freedom, self–sufficiency, and business go together. Responsible for their own welfare, in their own minds, at least, and ambitious, the frontiersmen sought land, ready mortgage money, public improvements—especially those facilitating access to markets—and beyond these, as little restraint on their operations as possible.[11] The formal characteristics of material existence at the frontier were entirely in tune with these aspirations. Cheap land, isolation, a simple technology, and abundance combined to offer an environment in which the pioneer's ideals made sense. All that was needed in addition were profitable markets and a right to sell without interference.

Education and religion serve a special purpose on the frontier. Through them a moral code was formulated, impressed upon the young, and reiterated to the old—a moral code that made existence possible in the anxiety–inspiring milieu of the frontier. As W. W.

---

10. Pierson, *loc. cit., New England Quarterly,* p. 234.
11. Hicks, *op. cit.,* p. 79, Burkhart, *op. cit.,* p. 74, and Craven, *Democracy,* p. 53.

Sweet points out in *Religion in the Development of American Culture,* these carriers of the community's conscience were of vital service in the battle against the ignorance, crudity, and indecency of frontier life. The schools worked to make Americans out of the children of the "others," to make them, one might say, regular people, and the churches were there to keep them that way. Through their combined moral effort they enabled the independent individuals of the atomic society to find a common basis for existence.

The typical frontier, then, as described initially by Frederick Jackson Turner and amplified by his many followers and critics is characterized: first, by agriculture, a low population density, and spatial isolation; second, by an economic system founded on simple productive techniques that provide abundantly, thereby encouraging self–sufficiency and equality; third, and here we find an explicit contradiction, by individuals who are reputed to be self–assertive, self–reliant, enthusiastic, and, at the same time, lacking in trust and inclined to conformity; and fourth, by weak traditional ties binding individuals into conventional patterns of action. As a result, associations are voluntary rather than customary and are designed for limited, specific operations. The general society erected on this voluntaristic base consisted of political, religious, educational, and economic institutions favoring the principle of freedom.

Ideally, the frontier society was formed of independent individuals. Such individuals were socially homogeneous—that is, relatively equal in status, one to the other—and belonged to households. Normally they operated separately but, from time to time and of their own free will, they formed groups founded on agreements common to all and designed for the completion of specific tasks. They formed such associations when and only when a task lay beyond the capacity of the separate interested parties. In short, frontier society was primarily a matter of providing a place where independence was maximized and where freedom could be made to work.

With this ideal–type model of frontier society as our guide we will now turn to a descriptive study of the countryside around the landing place of Nyack, New York, to investigate, firstly, the extent to which frontier society was realized there and, secondly, what happened after urbanism developed in a mild way at certain localities in that rural countryside.

3
THE SETTING

To situate ourselves, let us first take a hypothetical trip. Turn to Map I and, beginning at New York City, drive north along the Thomas E. Dewey Thruway towards Albany. For the first twenty miles or so the superhighway traverses wealthy Westchester County and then, near Tarrytown, it sweeps west to cross the Hudson River. At that point the river has widened into a great bay which is called the Tappan Zee.

On the eastern shore of the Zee we are in the world of Washington Irving. To our right, as we approach the Hudson, lies Sleepy Hollow, where the headless horseman rode. Tarrytown nestles along the riverbank close to the bridge. There, sometime towards the end of the seventeenth century, the patroon Frederick Philipse built his manor. During the early days of New York he was a man of great importance, a friend of several governors, and through his connections he had acquired much land. To all and sundry he and his fellow patroons on the Hudson's eastern shore were feudal lords. They were men of great power and authority in the Province of New York and sought to establish a peasant cultivation in Westchester and the counties to the north and to introduce an aristocratic way of life there. In keeping with this sentiment, Philipse, as Lord of the Manor of Philipsburg, had thrones erected in the church at Sleepy Hollow for himself and his dame.

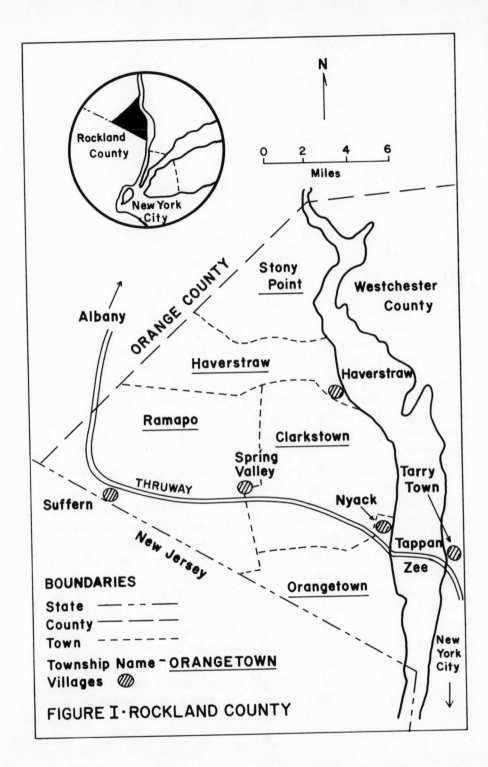

N

Rockland County

New York City

0 2 4 6
Miles

Albany

ORANGE COUNTY

Stony Point

Westchester County

Haverstraw

Haverstraw

Ramapo

Clarkstown

Spring Valley

Tarry Town

THRUWAY

Nyack

Suffern

New Jersey

Tappan Zee

Orangetown

New York City

BOUNDARIES

State —·—·—·—

County — — —

Town – – – –

Township Name – <u>ORANGETOWN</u>

Villages ⊘

FIGURE I·ROCKLAND COUNTY

Our destination, however, lies to the west, on the other shore of the Tappan Zee. Crossing the bridge we enter Rockland, a tight little county tucked between the Hudson River and New Jersey's northern border. If we were to turn off the road at the river's edge we would be in the Nyacks, three compact villages that press against the bank of the river at that point. If, on the other hand, we continue west, we enter Clarkstown. To the left is the township of Orangetown, and to the right, Haverstraw, which is both a village and a town. A few miles farther along, while still in Rockland County, we leave Clarkstown and enter the township of Ramapo, passing the small city of Spring Valley. At the village of Suffern, some twelve miles from the Tappan Zee, the superhighway turns north and following the course of the Ramapo River enters a mountain pass. Approximately five miles above the turn at Suffern, while still in the mountains, the road leaves Rockland and enters Orange, the next New York county to the north.

Rockland, rock–strewn and glacier–torn, is aptly named. The land is rough, often awkward, in its structure and defies efficient planning. In shape, the county is triangular, with an edge facing east, abutting the Hudson, and a point at its western extremity. In land area, Rockland is the smallest county in upstate New York.

During the early period of settlement in Rockland the nature of its boundaries discouraged travel into and through the county. Easy access was blocked on all sides. The Palisades, an igneous sill standing two to eight hundred feet above the Hudson River, form a precipitous cliff along its western bank and hinder travel from the Tappan Zee. Except at Nyack, where they draw back half a mile or so and create a shelf of land, and at Piermont, where a deep cut in their conformation exists, the Palisades are exceedingly difficult to mount from the river side.

The northwestern boundary of the county is lost in the stubby little Ramapos, a wasteland of small mountains and treacherous swamps. Over most of their reach these mountains have always discouraged communication between Rockland and the country to the north. In fact, prior to the Revolution, Rockland and Orange, the next county to the north, formed a single county called Orange. Difficulties following from the compartmentalization forced by the Ramapo Mountains led in 1798 to the formation of Rockland as a separate county. Only one place suitable for roads penetrates the Ramapos. This is the pass mentioned above, cut by the Ramapo River, where the Thruway, as before it, the Erie Railroad, turns upstate. It is located at the westernmost part of the county.

To the southwest is the border between the states of New York and New Jersey. Jealous of their prerogatives, these two states have naturally favored their own constituents above their neighbors when improving transportation and communication. As a result, the roads they built tended to run parallel to the boundary line, not across it. In fact, today's Thruway, built as recently as 1954, is itself an example of this kind of thinking.

European settlement in Rockland began in the late seventeenth century, when the first pioneers came there alone or in pairs and located at convenient landings along the Hudson. The three most popular locations were Nyack, Haverstraw, and Piermont (then called Tappan Landing), because of certain geographical advantages each possessed. At that time Indians still resided here and there throughout the county, and the first settlements were primarily posts for the Indian trade. The names of all three of these landings have Indian roots: Haverstraw and Tappan refer to local tribal groups and the word Nyack probably relates to the area's use as a fishing place by the aborigines. Together, they suggest that a close association existed between the earliest settlers and the Indians.

Only a few years later the first homestead farmers came to the county to settle. Sometime around 1682 a survey party, representing a group of fifteen farmers from the nominally Dutch settlements on Manhattan Island and in East New Jersey, ventured into the inland wilderness and bought a large tract of land from the Tappan Indians.[1] Identified in the original deed as Old Tappan and again, as the Christian Patented Lands, this tract lay in the meadows and swamps behind the Palisades and straddled what was eventually to be the boundary between New York and New Jersey. Rights to this deed, together with special provisions defining political authority in the then open surrounding territory, were confirmed by a patent granted in 1686 by Governor Dongan of New York as well as by the proprietors of East New Jersey.

---

1. Budke, "The History of the Tappan Patent," *Rockland Record*, II (1931-32), pp. 35-50.

The pioneers had not waited for such confirmation, however, and extant records indicate that some of the patentees had already moved to Tappan by 1684. Once there they organized as a congregation—Dutch Reformed—and began the distribution of the land among the several families. Operating under authority vested in them by the Province of New York they also established government, erecting the town and county of Orange. On their chosen plots they built rough cabins for themselves and their large families. These first habitations were often only burrows excavated in the side of a hill, lined with bark, and faced with upright posts set in the earth. Some were simple huts made of interwoven saplings and covered with bark.[2] As their farms prospered in the half century following, they built permanent houses of the indigenous red sandstone they quarried from nearby outcroppings. The land in Rockland at that time was very damp and swampy, and such farming as was possible was limited to the side hills.

By 1700 no more than two to three hundred people were homesteading in Rockland. The heaviest concentrations were still at the Hudson landings and on the Tappan Patent lands. The new century, however, brought with it a steady influx of colonists. While several, such as William Merritt, formerly Mayor of New York City, and Judge William Smith, were men of substance in the province, the great majority of the settlers in Rockland were persons of humble means. Exploitation on a centralized basis was not practical and neither plantation nor manorial agriculture took root there.

The Tappan Patent was an anomaly in that it had been granted to a group of ordinary farmers. Conventionally, provincial governors rewarded those they were indebted to for services rendered with large parcels of "vacant" land. These grants—in legal terminology, patents—contained thousands of acres and specified a token quit-rent.[3] Preferring the cosmopolitan life of the city, these patentees rarely settled on the land they had acquired in this manner. Instead, they turned their property into cash by subdividing the patents and selling off sections separately to individuals or to small groups. These second owners were the actual pioneers. Generally, the subdivisions they acquired were quite generous in size, ranging from two hundred

2. Green, *History of Rockland,* p. 10.
3. Cochran, *New York in the Confederation,* p. 105.

to a thousand acres, and provided land for several sons and their families as well as for the paterfamilias himself.

Many local writers stress the Dutch ancestry of the early settlers in Rockland and frequently leave the reader with the impression that Hollanders alone came there, but this is not correct. Actually, the county population had its roots in many ethnic groups, even prior to the Revolution. There were numerous Dutch, of course, from Manhattan, Harlem, East New Jersey and from the feudal domains of Westchester, but there were also free Negroes from Greenwich Village, English colonials from Long Island and New England, Scots and Irish, Germans from the Palatinate, and Huguenots from France. In cultural terms, the Dutch influence was strong and encouraged the impression of Dutchness in the heterogeneous people. The Dutch language was commonly spoken in Rockland until 1820, and for many years religious life there was dominated by the Reformed Church at Tappan. In addition, as large families were the rule and children of these families usually married the offspring of neighboring households, bloodlines and ethnic origins tended to merge. Consequently, the dominant group grew more influential as everyone, to some degree, participated in its membership.

Settlement continued throughout the eighteenth century and eventually the vacant land was occupied. But the pace of settlement was never even; there were surges of activity and long periods of quiescence. The Revolution, especially, interfered with land development in Rockland. By the time the war began, available land in the eastern two-thirds of the county had been taken by homesteaders. The original proprietors had been paid off, title had been established, and, generally, the land was in productive use. On the other hand, much of the western third of the county was still uninhabited. In an effort to secure a political advantage directly prior to the war, the provincial governor issued patents assigning these lands to several of his supporters—patents which were subsequently annulled by the newly constituted Assembly of the state. These lands then reverted to public domain. Nevertheless, and despite the absence of adequate title, a number of farmers maintained homesteads on these lands. In time, after much legal maneuvering, a large number of the squatters acquired absolute rights to the lands they were working. Simultaneously, others new to the area purchased, from government agents, title to land that was still vacant, and settled their families there. This complex process of reassignment and litigation continued for a considerable period following the war, but was in a large measure complete by the beginning of the nineteenth century.

The Revolution also had its impact on eastern Rockland. Throughout the war the county was an active theater of military operations and suffered considerably. The soil was blighted and the development of agriculture received a setback. Lawless bands called "cowboys" roamed the countryside and raised general havoc. The militia was called into service at inconvenient times and for protracted periods. Local residents were often uncertain as to whom they should support and as a result were vulnerable to the demands and depredations of antagonists from both sides. A number of the more prosperous farmers cast their lot too precisely with the British and, consequently, were divested of their holdings and forced to remove to Nova Scotia when the war was over. The farms of others were overrun by marauding troops, often more than once, and their fields and equipment badly damaged. Bottom land which had been drained and had become productive was allowed to return to swamp. Those who lived near these swamps permitted their farm animals to run loose in order to protect them from pillagers. As a result of the dislocation and destruction of the war extensive restoration and reorganization were necessary in its aftermath. It is difficult now to estimate how long this period of restoration lasted but, by all the evidence, the turmoil originating in the Revolutionary War had ended by 1800 and tranquillity again prevailed.

By the end of the eighteenth century, then, the Rockland frontier—meaning abundant land available for development—was closed. During that century the wilderness had been tamed and most of the potentially arable land put under cultivation. The Rockland countryside had, where practical, been cut up into freeholdings of moderate size. The settlers on these freeheld farms had cleared the land of forest, drained many of the swamps, and driven the wolves and panthers back into the mountains. Houses and barns had been built and roughcast roads laid among them. The first crops had been planted and harvested in the virgin soil, and where the soil had proved productive, crops had been planted again in succeeding seasons. Stores, mills, and smithies had begun operations, a local government had been organized, and churches and schools had been built. Although the process of settlement had been much prolonged because of an indifferent provincial land policy and the disruptive war, it was finally brought to completion. By 1800, some hundred years after the coming of the first pioneers, a simple agrarian economy was operating throughout Rockland County.

In Chapter 2 we defined the frontier in operational terms, beginning with an emphasis on open land and spatial isolation. As an abstraction the frontier implied abundant land held in clear title, a low density of population, and an isolation enforcing social distance. It was further argued there that these circumstances promoted self–sufficiency and that it was this self–sufficiency that produced the characteristic frontiersman and his unique society. While presenting the model of the frontier we did not provide a description of frontier space nor did we offer any estimate as to the time span of the frontier. In so doing we conformed to the conventions of standard literature on the subject, which tends towards generality and treats the frontier as an area devoid of character both in time and in space.

With respect to space, the standard approaches treat frontier areas as if they were homogeneous, neglecting the influence that differentiated land forms might have on developments within the areas. The fact that frontier theory evolved from midwestern examples may well account for such abstract approaches, as the land there is relatively featureless. A corollary of these approaches would be that space alone, as distance, guarantees isolation; consequently, population densities must be very low if frontier characteristics are to develop and be re-enforced. Otherwise, people would meet and greet, condone and condemn, and impose on each other. As long as one's neighbor is half a day's walk away, he is not likely to be much trouble.

When Turner and others discuss a time span, the stress is on the word "moment," which suggests that the frontier period was assumed to be relatively short; certainly not much longer than a generation.[4]

---

4. Professor Curti in his study of Trempealeau, Wisconsin, gives some indication of what he thinks may be an appropriate time span for the frontier period. Settlement began in the county area there in 1836. It was still sparsely settled in 1850 when the first federal census was taken. Population increased rapidly during the next twenty years. Curti dates the end of the frontier at Trempealeau, that is, the date when the "moment" has passed, as some time between 1869 and 1880. In all, the lapsed time is somewhat longer than thirty years. Cf. Curti, *American Community*, pp. 5-16, especially p. 7.

This time period, while short and definite, was also homogeneous in the sense that nothing of major importance occurred. A span of time one generation in length makes sense in that it allows individuals who have been socialized in frontier circumstances to mature and to assume important roles in the community. As such they more certainly would be products of the tradition–loosening process enforced by frontier experience than their fathers, who could hardly be expected to shuck off entirely the cultural impedimenta they had brought to the frontier, however much they might wish to.

Let us return to eighteenth–century Rockland and, with these strictures in mind, examine the settlement process there. First, and unlike the ideal frontier, the land there is anything but featureless. Its confining boundaries and its conformation, badly torn by diastrophic and glacial processes, define a situation in which space is singularly segmented and communication routes are ditched and diked and channeled into awkward circumvolutions. The many hills, streams, and swamps discouraged social intercourse and favored isolation within neighborhood compartments. The available land was never abundant, for approximately one–third of the acreage was mountain land and unsuitable for agrarian development. Time also had its events and lacked the homogeneity assumed for the frontier model. The Revolutionary War was a major factor, disrupting the process of settlement in the West and disorganizing the East. An indifferent land policy offered opportunity for other disrupting events and contributed to the lack of homogeneity.

In theory the Rockland population had reached the frontier saturation point of two to six persons per square mile by 1738 when the state reported a population of 1,484 persons there.[5] The use of gross densities, however, involves us in a fallacy of composition, for most of that population was concentrated in Orangetown, a township containing only one–seventh of the surface of the county. The density there was 33.6 persons per square mile, while the remaining six–sevenths, then known as the Haverstraw Precinct, reported

5. O'Callaghan, *Documentary History of New York,* IV, p. 185, reports the population. Paxson and Vance, *op. cit.,* pp. 500-505, suggest the defining densities. Were Curti to have used the two-to-six-per-square-mile limits to define the frontier period in Trempealeau, it would have been reduced to five years there. The density for that county was .6/sq. mi. in 1855, 3.4 in 1860, and by 1865, it had grown to 7.0/sq. mi. In 1880, the date Curti chose for the termination of the frontier, the county density was 22.6 persons per square mile. Curti, *op. cit.,* p. 6-7.

a density of 4.4. While it is impossible at this date to make a firm statement about distribution within the Haverstraw Precinct, it is probable that most of the population was concentrated close to the Hudson River and that a general figure for population density again distorts the situation. Fifty years later, in 1790—the year in which the first Federal census was taken—the computed density for Orangetown had risen to 47.2 persons per square mile, while that for the Haverstraw Precinct was 32.7.[6]

Let us consider what the 1790 densities would mean in terms of the actual location of individuals in a township. The average size of a Rockland household in 1712 was 6.8 persons,[7] and in 1790, 6.0 persons. Slaves are included in these computations of household size. If we take the lower of the two figures (6.0 per household), determine the number of households, and then distribute these households evenly over the area, we find that in Orangetown, where the population concentration is heaviest (47.2 persons per square mile in 1790), there would be approximately eight households for each square mile of area. In other words, the several households would be a little over a third of a mile from each other. Of course, Rockland geography does not allow for such an even distribution, and there would be many localities where houses were much closer and others where they would be more distant.

Again assuming even distribution, if these households were devoted entirely to farming, each would have been supported by a farm of some 80 acres. With one–third of the land unsuitable for crops, the effective farm size would have been around fifty acres. This analysis suggests that fifty acres of arable land would have been sufficient for the support of a household of some six persons in Rockland in 1790, a date at which trade routes to the outside had not yet been developed to any marked extent.

The extant fragment of an assessment roll for the Town of Ramapo (then called New Hempstead) for 1807, published in Volume III of the *Rockland Record,* a compendium of historical material about the county, gives us an impression of the Rockland tenure structure as it actually existed towards the end of the frontier period. This fragment is the only record known from the agrarian period in which

6. *Heads of Families at the First Census of the United States Taken in the Year 1790, New York,* pp. 140-142, 146-7.
7. "1712 Census," *Rockland Record,* II (1931-32), pp. 21-24.

the assessor kept his accounts in real quantities rather than in value quantities, and includes the assessments on approximately one–third of the land suitable for agriculture in the township. One hundred four householders were assessed in this listing, of whom 95 owned one or more acres of farm land. Persons assessed but not owning land were not necessarily poor. Several owned horses, oxen, or cows, while a tavern owner was one of the most influential men in the county. Two others, who were not residents of the county, owned large plots described as "undeveloped mountain land."

The median size of farm plots was 59 acres. Only three exceeded 200 acres, and only ten had more than 125 acres. Two–thirds of the farms had reported between 25 and 125 acres. Eighty–six plots were owned by persons resident in Ramapo and nine by non–residents. From all indications the resident owners farmed their acreage. All in all, then, we find farm land, as assessed in Ramapo in 1807, distributed relatively evenly among the several holders with a standard plot close to the fifty acres anticipated. Except for undeveloped mountain land, no exceptionally large plots were reported, nor were plots segmented into many disjunct small units as was characteristic of European manors. Instead, while the plot size was much smaller and the population density greater than the Turner model would indicate, the characteristic frontier form with households located on individual plots at a distance from each other had been achieved, at least in Ramapo. There is no evidence that the situation differed markedly in other areas of the county.

Withal, however, experience in Rockland during the frontier period ran counter to that indicated by the Turner model in two important ways. For one, the time span during which the land was being settled continued much longer than had been anticipated. One hundred twenty years—hardly a Turner "moment"— had elapsed before the land was filled completely, a period during which four to five generations had come to maturity. Conventionally, newer generations settled close to the original family home or, if they migrated, it was to the very near west, into the hinterlands of Rockland where they joined men and women new to the area as pioneers. In effect, the great majority of the new settlers in Clarkstown and Ramapo in the late part of the eighteenth century were not far from home nor from the cultural influence of the paternal homestead, and the word "diffusion" describes more precisely than does "migration" the process of settlement in the western sections of the county.

As one example, let us take those households in which the head of the household was named Blauvelt, the name most common among early county residents. All persons with this name are direct descendants of a single individual, Hendrick Gerritsen, originally a Dutch farmer on Manhattan Island, and later a shareholder in the Tappan Patent.[8] Hendrick, who was called Blauvelt (which means "blue field" and was taken to be descriptive of his Manhattan farm) was the father of many sons. In the census of 1712, eight of the 42 households in Orangetown were headed by Blauvelts (19.1% of the total). In 1790, Orangetown reported 190 households, of which 33 were headed by Blauvelts (17.6%). Haverstraw Precinct, which had had 17 households in 1712, reported 810 households in 1790, including 21 whose head was named Blauvelt (2.6% of the Haverstraw households). Thus, over three–quarters of a century, the Blauvelt family had maintained its dominant position in Orangetown while expanding into the Haverstraw Precinct.

The diffusion process continued into the nineteenth century. In 1820, a date prior to the time villages appear in Rockland County, Orangetown reported 43 Blauvelt households out of 329 (13.1%), while the townships of Clarkstown, Haverstraw, and Ramapo, previously known as the Haverstraw Precinct, reported 39 Blauvelt households out of a total of 1,246 (3.1%). Thirty–one of the 39 were located in Clarkstown, that part of the old precinct closest to Orangetown.[9]

Although no other family approached the Blauvelts in the number of household units, many of the larger ones showed a similar pattern. They expanded into the western reaches of the county while simultaneously retaining an important position in the older settlements. It follows, then, from this evidence of localized diffusion, that the sharp disruption in custom's bounds which Turner indicates as characteristic of the frontier probably did not take place in Rockland. What seems more likely is that migration into and throughout the county developed gradually over an extended period of time.

In such a pattern traditions would maintain their grip as they

8. Budke, "Hendrick Gerritsen Blauvelt," *Rockland Record*, II (1931-32), p. 45.
9. *Manuscripts of U.S. Census, 1820 — Rockland County, New York.*

spread from household to household, but their force would diminish with the passage of time. The reasons for this diminution would lie with cultural contact and assimilation as well as with the frontier–type material situation offered in Rockland. When the sons and daughters of the Tappan Dutch moved west, they would encounter the English who were then located north of today's Spring Valley, or the Palatines who had settled in the Ramapos, in addition to others who were products of still different traditions. At the same time new people, from both inside and outside the county, were constantly moving in among the old Dutch of Orangetown. With individuals from all these tradition–bearing systems in contact, one could expect transformations, both subtle and direct, in the dominant system. As such transformations took place slowly, it might well have seemed to the settlers themselves that tradition was actually being conserved rather than transformed.

A second important way in which the Rockland experience differed importantly from that anticipated in the frontier thesis concerns land tenure. Throughout the colonial period there was uncertainty with reference to land titles in Rockland. A primary source of this uncertainty was the boundary line between New York and New Jersey. While its azimuth direction was accepted early in the colonial period, its point of origin was always in doubt. At times this point was placed as far north as Haverstraw, and at others, as far south as today's Alpine, New Jersey. Numerous legal battles between the two provinces developed over this issue and it was not entirely resolved until 1774. Prior to that date a landholder could never be certain whether his farm was located in New York or New Jersey. As a guarantee for their title, many early settlers secured patents from both provinces and, in addition, arranged for the purchase of the property from resident Indians.

Furthermore, the patents granted by the New York governors were frequently poorly drawn. The Rockland pioneers, who were in most cases men of small means, often found that the boundaries of the property they had acquired were vague. Consequently, they were forced into complex and expensive litigation to protect their holdings. The Tappan Patentees, for example, were forced to defend in court their western boundary against encroachments by the holders of the south moiety of the Kakiat Patent, holders who were men of prominence in the colony. And, as indicated earlier, the Revolutionary War had its impact in compounding confusion. After hostilities had ended those who had been identified with the English cause were divested of their holdings, which were then redistributed, sometimes on a speculative basis. For all these reasons the secure title on which frontier self–reliance supposedly was founded cannot be said to have existed in Rockland.

When examined in terms of the frontier model, however, title ambiguity turns out to be paradoxical in its consequences. In contrast to Westchester and several other New York counties, Rockland over a period of time, was settled largely as a land of small farms held in fee simple. Muddled titles combined with a limited potential for profits to discourage large–scale operators. Instead, Rockland became a place for independent–minded men of simple means who sought to homestead beyond the reach of colonial authority. The county was also fortunate to have been intermittently subject to the administrative jurisdiction of New Jersey during the colonial period. The leaders of that colony were generally held to favor an enlightened land policy—one encouraging absolute ownership and small, manageable holdings as incentives to settlement in the colonial wilderness.[10] To some degree, then, the pattern of small farm freeholding which characterized Rockland by the end of the settlement period was a product of the prevailing title ambiguity. This same title ambiguity, however, also impeded the settlement process there and, consequently, contributed to the protracted length of the frontier period.

Over a time span extending from 1680 until after 1800, families had come to the rough and awkward land of Rockland to build their homes and to farm. Sons and grandsons, daughters and granddaughters, grew to maturity and stayed to work the old homesteads or moved to farms nearby to build lives for themselves and their families. Working separately and together for over a century they established an agrarian way of life, a ground of being on which a society could be founded. This, then, was their frontier "moment."

By American Midwestern standards these pioneers lived close

10. Mark, *Agrarian Conflicts*, p. 74, quotes Lord Bellomont, Governor of New York: "What man . . . will be such a fool as to become a base tenant to Mr. Delius, Colonel Schuyer, Mr. Livingston . . . when, for crossing Hudson's River that man can for a song purchase a good freehold in the Jerseys."

to one another—too close, in fact, to be able to ignore their kin groups entirely and the dependency lodged in these groups. Also, the moment during which settlement took place was exceedingly protracted in length and offered many opportunities for continued association across generational lines. So, old ways persisted and interpenetrated the new. Nevertheless, and despite the absence of a sharp break with the past, a new way of life was founded in Rockland, having its own special shape and force, and able to persist in the back country throughout much of the nineteenth century. That way of life had much about it that reminds us of the frontier thesis.

4

THE AGRARIAN ECONOMY

Economic conditions defined a simple and consistent pattern of existence in Rockland during the agrarian period. Until 1830 the settled portion of the county was devoted, in a great measure, to subsistence agriculture.[1] Extended family units, often owning slaves, lived in the red stone houses we still find scattered throughout the county. Goods production on the farms was largely organized on a household basis and directed, at least during the eighteenth century, towards obtaining a living from the soil. In conformity with the frontier thesis, such farm–households were, for most purposes, self–sufficient economic units.

Beyond the individual household there existed a primitive division of economic function based, in general, on direct trading among several households. Lacking currency, the households exchanged services and commodities on a barter basis, keeping their accounts in cash terms. Until 1830 the conventional standard of value in the back country of Rockland was pounds, shillings, and pence, with two shillings being worth 25 cents when equivalencies were necessary.

---

1. With one important exception: iron mining and smelting was carried on in the Ramapo Mountains from 1736 on. An extensive establishment for the working of iron products was developed at Ringwood, on the New Jersey side of the state boundary, between 1764 and 1767 by Peter Hasenclever. Hasenclever's operations extended throughout the Ramapos and were continued by others after his return to Europe. Cf. Ransom, *Vanishing Ironworks*, pp. 17-52.

On the whole the farmers' requirements were simple and in most cases could be satisfied either at the farm itself or through trading and sharing with the neighbors.[2]

Only after the turn of the century, when the means of transport and communication to and from the metropolitan center at New York had been developed and when a market for cash crops had appeared there, were Rockland's farmers able to shift many of their operations to a cash basis. John W. Ferdon, writing in Cole's *History of Rockland* in 1884, dates the change from a pure subsistence system to a cash, market–oriented system as 1813 when, he reports, Rockland farmers began raising Merino sheep for wool. He maintains that Rocklanders had "devoted themselves almost exclusively to the pursuit of agriculture" (by which he means subsistence farming) for the first 150 years of settlement.

There were no real hamlets in Rockland during the rural period, no aggregates of households where people intermingled and worked and lived in close conjunction. Hostile Indians do not seem to have been a problem and the Rocklanders did not build stockades for protection. Commerce, the other important reason for crowding together, was not developed. Thus, lacking incentives to build in tight villages, the Rockland pioneers located their houses at their separate farms, wherever the site was dry and provided good access and sunlight. Thus they saved themselves a good deal of walking to and from the fields they farmed.

For an example of the Rockland settlement pattern let us turn to a neighborhood in the western area of Orangetown, commonly referred to as Sickeltown.[3] Map II, on page 42, is offered as a guide to places and names for this study. A number of families, including the Sickels, the Kuypers, the Perrys, and the Oblenis settled beside the trail running north along the west bank of the Hackensack River

2. Haring, *Floating Chips*, p. 13. ". . . their chief concern was to manage affairs so to be as independent as possible from avoidable outlay of money. Hence economy was strictly enforced and luxuries of certain kinds rigidly excluded." Dr. Haring was a direct descendant of the Tappan Patentees of Orangetown and grew up in the Northern Valley (Bergen County) area of New Jersey in a locale contiguous to Rockland. *Floating Chips* contains his reminiscences of life in the back country in 1830-40. Bailey, *Pre-Revolutionary Dutch Houses*, p. 35, says Rockland and Bergen were "thoroughly akin."

3. As used here the word "town" was often applied to localities without regard to political definition. The first county seat, which was comprised of a courthouse, a church, the parish manse, a tavern, and three farmhouses, was called Tappantown. Militia training took place at Middletown, a convenient field halfway along the road between two of the more settled areas.

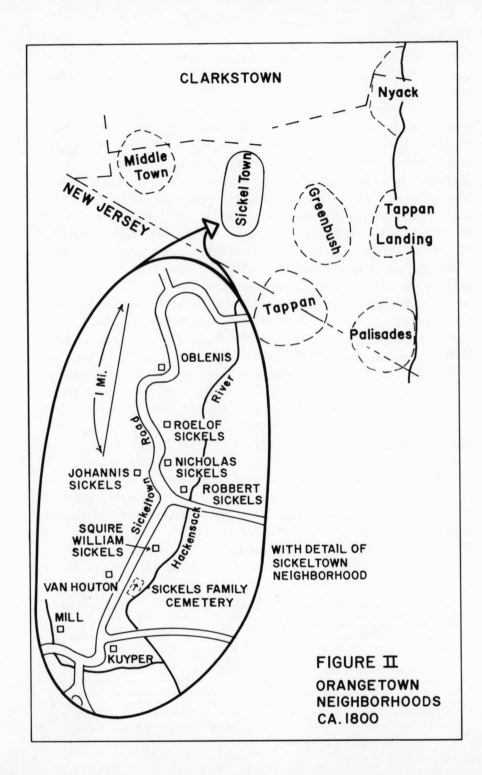

CLARKSTOWN

Nyack

Middle Town

NEW JERSEY

Sickel Town

Greenbush

Tappan Landing

Tappan

Palisades

1 Mi.

OBLENIS

River

ROELOF SICKELS

Road

NICHOLAS SICKELS

JOHANNIS SICKELS

Sickeltown

ROBBERT SICKELS

Hackensack

SQUIRE WILLIAM SICKELS

WITH DETAIL OF SICKELTOWN NEIGHBORHOOD

VAN HOUTON

SICKELS FAMILY CEMETERY

MILL

KUYPER

FIGURE II

ORANGETOWN NEIGHBORHOODS CA. 1800

during the 1730s. Of these, we will concentrate on the Sickels, the family which eventually gave the trail and its vicinity their name.[4] To this day the road there is called Sickeltown Road.

The Sickels were descendants of one Zacharias Sickels, who may have been an Austrian from Vienna. A soldier of fortune, he had been in the service of the Privileged West India Company (Dutch) in Curacao. In 1655 he was transferred to New Amsterdam and subsequently was attached to the garrison at Fort Orange (Albany). While at Fort Orange Zacharias secured his discharge from military service and settled nearby to raise a family. He worked there as a carpenter.

Willem Sickels, his grandson, was a Rockland pioneer. In 1732 he married Elizabeth Kuyper, a New Jersey girl and most likely a relative of a Nyack family of the same name. The Kuypers were the original patentees of Nyack and played active roles in the development of inland Rockland during its earliest period. Through this connection with the Kuyper family, Willem Sickels acquired 100 acres in the western section of Orangetown. This land, a swampy, sidehill plot abutting on the west bank of the Hackensack River, was part of the "expense lot" of the Kakiat Patent. To provide funds for the surveying of that Patent, a large tract located in the center of Rockland, a parcel of 1,000 acres, called the "expense lot," had been set aside for sale.

Cornelius Kuyper of Nyack had acquired two–thirds of the lot, and a son of his had already settled on its southern section when Willem Sickels, his wife, and their two children moved there to their 100–acre plot in 1737. A survey of the land suggests that they probably came by boat, paddling up the Hackensack from New Jersey, and on reaching their property, turned up a small draw that looked inviting and beached their craft. Nearby, on a spot of high ground standing above the draw and convenient to a generous spring where watercress still grows abundantly, they built a rude cabin, their first house. As the years passed, Willem and Elizabeth Sickels became the parents of seven sons and five daughters.

Vigorous in business matters too, Willem extended his holdings until he had acquired the entire thousand–acre expense lot, either by inheritance or by purchase. With his son, Robbert, who remained a bachelor, father Willem operated a farm of some 200 acres

4. Cf. Bailey, *Pre-Revolutionary Dutch Houses*, pp. 188-9, 202-9, and 225-7, for information on the Sickels and *passim* for other families in the neighborhood.

located near the center of the lot. Those of his sons who survived to adulthood and married cleared extensive sections of the remainder of the lot and built homes convenient to their farms. At the time of the 1790 census, three of the brothers and a nephew were farming at Sickeltown and were among the more prosperous men of Orangetown. They operated contiguous farms and their houses were set approximately a third of a mile along the trail paralleling the Hackensack. Together, the four households, with some 1,000 acres in all, supported 43 individuals, of whom 18 were slaves. The largest of these households was William's, the fifth brother, with sixteen members, seven being slaves. William—Squire William to be precise—was recorded in 1796 as having the fourth highest property assessment in Orangetown, and his oldest brother, Robbert, the fifth highest.

In 1810 five Sickels households were reported in the federal census. Robbert's farm had been split in two, with one half operated by a Sickels and the other by a nephew with a different name, making six farms in all where there had been four in 1790. These six farms supported 40 persons, of whom 11 were slaves and three, free Negroes. Two of the brothers still survived at that date.

As the many sons and daughters of this family grew to adulthood, the standard pattern was for them to marry into neighboring families and to settle in the vicinity of their parents' farms, often on land their fathers owned. Where land was abundant, as was the case with the Sickels brothers, the Tappan Patentees, and many others of the original pioneers, the common practice was for the recently married couple to build a new house "down the road a piece," and after clearing the land around their place to set to work there to raise crops and children. Chances were that the young couple acquired legal title to their homestead only some years after they had begun working it. In the common understanding it was theirs, however, and all that the formal division of the property did was to ratify an existing fact.

During the eighteenth and early nineteenth centuries this proliferation of family households seems to have been the typical pattern to neighborhood development in Rockland. At Greenbush (today's Blauvelt) we find Smith and Blauvelt houses, and at Palisades, the Sneden houses. Again and again, the houses of the children are located somewhere near those of their parents. Where a new name appears in any neighborhood it generally turns out to be that of a son–in–law to the stem family. In a dynamic sense, the original households grew large and then segmented by way of marriage. This process could continue as long as there was open land in the family plot and by all indications was still operating in eastern Rockland as late as 1800. When land became scarce, of course, and the family plot was fully utilized, a new household unit had to move elsewhere to a new neighborhood.

The general neighborhood, a sort of integrated superhousehold of interdependent and somewhat related family units, operated as a secondary economic entity, satisfying needs which could not be provided for at the primary level of the homestead. This neighborhood entity was united by kinship and by the sharing and trading of specialized skills. Each adult member of the several families took on some special function necessary to the continued existence and prosperity of the neighborhood. Living within walking distance of each other, they traded their services as needed, performing specialties according to their talents. The older man, with his long experience in local affairs, often became an informal practical lawyer, mediating conflicts and drawing legal papers. The apt pupil filled in as schoolmaster during the slow season, and the enterprising individual set up a store or smithy in his farmhouse.

Sickeltown was such a neighborhood with its simple, but developed, division of labor at this secondary level. Rulof Van Houten, a son–in–law of Squire William's, found he had a fine mill site on Nauraushaun Creek and erected a gristmill there. Robbert, father Willem's eldest son, built most of his brother's houses, constructing them of the red sandstone he quarried from an outcropping on the bank of the Hackensack River. In addition, he assumed responsibility for dividing up the family holdings among his brothers and nephews. Johannis Sickels, the fourth brother, who had built his house to the west of the road away from the river, ran a shop in his house, and Squire William served as Justice of the Peace for Orangetown. One of the Sickels (a local antique dealer does not specify which) made furniture for his neighbors. His work is highly regarded to this day.

Two diaries, left to posterity by chance, provide us with a closer description of the rural economy in Rockland than can be drawn from the Sickeltown material. Unfortunately, both are set rather late in the period. The diarists were men who had been born in the back country during colonial times and who had farmed there but who were also active in commercial developments at the Hudson River landings. Essentially, they are transitional persons, not truly representative of the rural period, for they had alternatives to the self–sufficient homestead life. The diaries, however, are concerned with their agrarian activities. The author of the first was Tunis Smith of the Greenbush neighborhood (later, of Nyack village);[5] Nicholas Gesner, a farmer who made his home in the Palisades neighborhood, wrote the second.[6]

Smith, who spent his childhood and early manhood at Green-bush (Blauvelt), has left an account of his experiences while resident there. He was born in 1772 on the family farm. His father, Isaac P. Smith, had received his home and land by inheritance from the paternal grandfather, Petrus, a descendant of the Tappan Patentees, and, in fact, the farm was a part of the family share in that Patent. During his childhood Tunis attended common school and then, when he was about thirteen, learned the weaver's trade. It is possible that he learned this trade from his grandfather, as Petrus Smith also was a weaver. Until he was sixteen Tunis worked at this trade and on the farm. Then, in 1788, he went back to school, but this time as schoolmaster rather than as student.[7] He taught school off and on for the two years following and then gave up school-teaching as an occupation.

For a short period Smith worked and wove again as before. Then, in 1792, when he was twenty years old, he learned surveying (in seven weeks, he says). Following this short course of study he devoted his energies, at different times, to one or another of his various occupations. As a farmer he raised flax, wheat, rye, and buck-wheat. In addition, he cut timber, and in 1795 in association with his father, Isaac, he built a mill. Between 1795 and 1802 Tunis tended this mill for halves with his father.

In 1802, Isaac divided the farm in a tentative way, granting to

---

5. Tunis Smith, *Diary,* handwritten, with Salisbury family papers at the Tappan Zee Historical Museum, Orangeburg, N.Y.
6. Nicholas Gesner, *Diary,* handwritten, Palisades, N.Y., Public Library. A third diary, covering approximately one year, c. 1800, by David Pye is in the Budke Collection, New York Public Library, Item §87. Pye lived in Clarkstown, near New City.
7. By all indications Tunis Smith was an exceptionally able man. His handwriting is clear and precise, even graceful, and his extant map-work gives evidence of outstanding cartographical talent. See Budke and Christie, *Old Nyack,* p. 22, for a reproduction of one of his maps.

Peter, the younger son, the old farm and the use of the mill. Tunis's share was another farm located "near by" which Isaac also owned. In addition, Tunis was expected to help his brother with the flax. The income from the mill was set aside to provide for the parents.

Tunis stayed at Greenbush for eight years operating the "near by" farm. Then, in 1810, when he was 38 years old, he moved to Nyack where he embraced commercial enterprise, opened a store, and ended his connections with the old, rural way of life. Shortly afterwards his brother and his father followed him to Nyack to settle, and the ancestral farm was put out to different parties for shares. Several years later the Greenbush land was sold and passed from the control of the family altogether. The stage of activity for the Smiths had shifted from the back country to the village and a new drama was about to begin.

From this short account it can be seen that during his youth and early manhood, Tunis Smith never applied himself exclusively to any occupation. Generally, he can be described as a farmer with a flair for words and maps and also, as restless. He devoted the largest share of his time to obtaining a subsistence from the soil for himself and his family, and in this effort worked closely with his father and his brother. But in addition, as an able and industrious individual, he took advantage of the many and varied opportunities afforded by his environment. He was ambitious, too, and at the age of 38 he was willing to begin all over again in a new set of circumstances. Throughout, Tunis was his own man. His limits were defined by the potentials of the rural economy, by his talents and energy, and by the opportunities offered. There was no tangled web of approved precedent and institutional structure to restrain him, and within a modest range, given the energy, the means, and the desire, he could act as he saw fit. His world was his oyster. It was a small oyster, but what there was of it was pretty much his.

Nicholas Gesner, our second diarist, owned a farm that straddled the border between the states of New York and New Jersey at Palisades, a neighborhood located near the southeastern point of Rockland close by the Hudson River. From his diary, dated in the 1830s and '40s, we find that Gesner still lived in much the same manner as Tunis Smith had lived at Greenbush at the turn of the century.[8]

8. The Nicholas Gesner *Diary* is an extensive manuscript written in longhand, covering day-to-day activities for the years 1830-1853. Gesner seems to have

Gesner was born in 1765, well before the Revolution, and died in 1858 at the age of 92. He was the youngest son of one John Gesner, a German from Wurtenburg who had purchased land near Tappan in the 1730s and settled there. Nicholas spent his whole life in Rockland.[9] Throughout, he must have been an exceedingly sturdy individual; it is clear from his diary that he was active and involved in local matters until he was a very old man. In 1835, at the age of 70, he recorded the state census for Orangetown, travelling over most of his territory on foot while completing the survey. In his diary, an entry dated 1841 mentions walking from his home in Palisades to the Slote New Landing (Piermont) out of curiosity. He took the walk with a neighbor, he says, to view the railroad works standing at the end of the "long pier" at Piermont. These works, which had recently been completed, were designed to provide terminal services for the Erie Railroad which was then under construction in Rockland. The round trip between Palisades and Piermont is about five miles, and the grade is quite steep in one or two places along the road.

Nicholas Gesner was primarily a farmer. He devoted part of his efforts to subsistence production and the remainder to a cash crop which he sent to New York City in the care of his son, Jacob, for sale. Travel between the city and the various river landings in Rockland was already commonplace in the 1830s, when Gesner began writing in his diary, and farmers who lived near the landings had little difficulty arranging with boatmen to carry their produce to market. Among the crops Gesner produced for sale in New York were apples, raspberries, currants, and potatoes. He also gathered nuts and cut firewood.

In addition to his farming, Gesner served as surveyor, schoolteacher, and sometime lawyer for his neighbors. In his youth he had been a boatbuilder, and in 1836 when evil reports were being circulated about a boat then on the ways at Nyack, he was called there to inspect the hull and judge its seaworthiness. Gesner was also active politically and the party intermittently repaid him for his support

used the diary both as an account book and as a record of agreements. The description of his way of life offered herein has been reconstructed from the material contained in this diary. The manuscript of the diary, together with a typed summary by W. S. Gilman is available at the library in Palisades, New York.

9. He claims to have been present at the hanging of Major André at Tappan in 1780. Nicholas Gesner, *Diary*, Momento §16, July 19, 1834.

with patronage appointments such as the census work mentioned earlier. During the War of 1812 he saw service with the militia and eventually rose to the rank of Colonel. He served as trustee on the school board and, as a dedicated, articulate, and argumentative Methodist, he devoted much of his time to the "glorious work of God." Yet, respected and trusted with important neighborhood affairs as he was, he still had his practical community responsibilities. The 70–year–old patriarch was still obligated for his allotted two days a year of physical labor repairing the county roads. Some years he worked himself, along with his neighbors; in other years he lent his wagon in lieu of his physical presence.

In producing goods for market as well as for subsistence, the Gesner farm of the 1830s operated on a mixed currency basis involving both cash and barter. Often the cash was used to strike a balance in transactions primarily involving the barter of goods and services. A review of the Gesner accounts for three months (July–September, 1834) provides a description of his ordinary transactions.[10] In addition to the money he earned at the New York City farmers' market, Gesner received a cash income from his many school, surveying, and legal service activities. In partnership with Jacob Gesner he purchased clams and oysters from river fishermen and peddled them throughout the Palisades neighborhood. When funds were short Gesner borrowed from his more prosperous neighbors. Such loans seem to have been given for short terms at six percent with extensions possible should the need arise; they were formalized in writing. There were no banks in Rockland at the time.

Gesner's routine expenditures were chiefly for groceries to supplement the produce of his own farm, for farm and household equipment, for taxes, and for labor. Approximately half his expenditures for the three months were for groceries. Three rough categories can be discerned from an examination of the Gesner grocery list. First, there were the import products from overseas, including sugar, salt, tea, rice, molasses, and chocolate. According to the local historian, Dr. Frank Green, such goods were bartered for local products even during the earlier phase of the agrarian period, prior to the time

10. *Ibid.*, July 1, 1834 to September 28, 1834. Prior to this period the diary is too fragmentary to provide us with a running account and subsequently Gesner discontinued keeping accounts in the diary. For the three months his reported income was $6.41 and his expenses $13.52. He received no income at all during September. Conventionally, he kept his accounts in pounds, shillings, and pence.

when communication between Rockland and the city had been regularized. Cloth, butter, and eggs, for example, might be exchanged for tea, coffee, tobacco, sugar, and crockery. The second category of food routinely purchased was fish, which Gesner obtained from neighbors who owned land adjacent to the river and fished as well as farmed. Finally, Gesner also purchased beef and flour—indicating thereby the degree to which market–oriented farm production had already displaced subsistence production in his neighborhood by 1834.[11]

From time to time Gesner purchased farm tools and household equipment from local merchants. These were people who kept stores in their houses, which generally were located at points convenient to transport and communication, such as a river landing or next to a junction on the King's Highway. They also farmed. Over the three–month period in 1834 Gesner spent, for all purposes, a total of 106 shillings, nine pence. Of that sum, only fourteen shillings were spent on items other than food or labor. A scythe and material for repairing a chair comprised the largest part of these residual expenditures. In addition to purchases of farm tools and household equipment, Gesner also bought paper and numerous books for his library. These books seem to have been the only "luxury" items he bought. They were mainly on religious subjects and ordinarily were purchased from itinerant peddlers.

Other than food, labor was the most important expenditure item. Approximately one–third of Gesner's outlays from July through September paid for the labor of the hands on his farm. Included in the labor account were both cash and barter transactions. One such hand received four shillings (50 cents at the standard exchange rate) plus a half pint of rum for a day's work. For boy's work he paid a shilling a day. He hired his helpers by the day, or part thereof, and settled his accounts with them on either a daily or monthly basis. Such workers were often neighbors, farmers themselves, or farmers' sons; others were day laborers who worked from farm to farm regularly. Because Gesner was sick for approximately half of the three–month period, it is probable that his labor outlays

11. Haring, *op. cit.*, p. 16, maintains that every farmer in his neighborhood packed his own pork and beef. He also points out that rye was the leading cereal in the Rockland area. *Ibid.*, p. 13. Gesner, of course, was located close to the river and except for the Palisades cliff was in a position offering greater opportunities to earn cash than was the inland farmer.

were larger than normal. During his sickness work continued on the farm under the supervision of his son, Herbert, who lived nearby and was a cobbler by trade.

With the exception of property taxes, Gesner's other outlays involved payment in kind in one form or another. He carried his own Indian corn and rye to a nearby miller for milling. The miller's fee was set, in the one case reported, at one–tenth by weight of the total product. The farm also sent yarn to the weaver and fuller to be manufactured into cloth. In addition to maintaining the house, Gesner's wife, Gracie, spun the wool into yarn, supervised the cloth production, and kept chickens which she sent to New York for sale. Her accounts were often recorded separately from those of her husband.

Both Nicholas Gesner and Tunis Smith spent their lives in the gray area between two critical moments of social development. They were born into a society dominated by frontier–type economic relationships, that is, by subsistence farming carried on by relatively isolated households. During their lifetimes trade relationships with New York City expanded considerably and were formalized. These new relationships provided a major impetus to the development of village communities in Rockland later in the nineteenth century. The testimony of Smith and Gesner, however, is rooted in ordinary existence on back country farms.

In a practical sense their testimony argues that economic conditions in Rockland did operate to maintain functional equality among individuals. Previously, we pointed out that by the close of the agrarian period Rockland County land had been divided relatively equally among the settlers. Our examination of Sickeltown indicated that land there had been distributed through sectioning until a neighborhood pattern similar to that of Ramapo, albeit with larger farms, had been achieved. We also found that family relationships undoubtedly played a more important role in the maintenance of economic well–being than our study of the ideal frontier would indicate. At Sickletown open land from the paternal farm was granted to newly–formed family households as they came into existence. The oldest son helped his younger brothers get established. Tunis Smith worked closely in his endeavors with his father and brother, Nicholas Gesner with his sons. While Nicholas and his wife, Gracie, each concentrated on their own areas of work, the household product was the sum total of their efforts, and each stood to gain from the productive effort of the other. In an exact sense, then, none of these individuals was ever entirely self–sufficient; instead, they were always participants in a family–neighbor group. And, while it is likely that interdependence was less developed a generation or two earlier, the extant material from that period, especially when studied in terms of land distribution, suggests that such family–neighbor interdependencies were always present on the Rockland scene.

In support of this family–neighborhood interdependence both Gesner and Smith were specialists in certain tasks for their localities. Nevertheless, while their skill is often impressive, what is interesting is the range of their activities; it is just as reasonable to describe them as "jacks–of–all–trades" as "specialists."[12] Each performed many diverse tasks which were useful in their neighborhoods. In fact, the situation in Rockland during the agrarian period was made for the gifted amateur. With an abundance of problems to solve and few rules to go by, acumen and a native talent counted far more than credentials. Given this milieu, able, forceful men such as Smith and Gesner found many opportunities for the expression of their energy and imagination. In this sense the situation was encouraging.

The Rockland pioneer who held title to a farm and who combined intelligent application with hard work was almost certain to earn a direct compensation in increased productivity from his farm and in increased real income. Money set aside and invested in a new plow or churn returned rich dividends in work saved and in richer yields at harvest time. An hour saved from routine duties was an hour to spend draining marsh land or building a wagon. Such an hour was surplus for the busy farmer, an explicit saving, and available as time to be spent in some other manner. It made further investment possible. With so much to do and so much to be gained by doing, any saving that could be converted into improvements was worthwhile. For the backwoods farmer time saved out of the routine of existence was necessary if well–being was to be achieved at the homestead.

In the ill–formed, unsystematically integrated rustic economy each man's act of improvement was likely also to be his neighbor's gain. The reinvestment of saved energy or extra production by any

12. The same can be said for the third diarist, David Pye. Pye wrote deeds and wills, colored and pressed cloth in his mill, farmed, and repaired watches. He was also a surveyor, country lawyer, and often served in important elective offices. Cf. Pye, *Diary*, in Budke Collection, Item §87.

farmer for his own benefit extended the possible range of services offered in a neighborhood. Consequently, a farmer who applied himself industriously benefited not only himself but his whole neighborhood as well. Nicholas Gesner's wagon was available for special jobs on the county road or for transporting apples to the landing, and Tunis Smith's surveying skills were useful in the settlement of disputes among farmers. Their constructive efforts did not contribute to their own advantage alone—they also served their neighbors.

Enterprise in this milieu must have been good for one's self-respect. The neighborhood in which one lived comprised a small general public in whose presence one functioned, and it was that public that counted, not the opinions of an anonymous greater world. The neighborhood–public was founded on kinship, interdependency, and face–to–face acquaintanceship. It was not difficult for an individual to assess the social worth of an enterprise, or for his neighbor to do so either, if each was willing to be reasonable. Such assessment could be made in terms that made sense personally, for no esoteric knowledge was required so long as the matter under consideration involved the direct experience of everyday living in the neighborhood. Farming and clearing, milling and weaving, praying and organizing were activities close to nature and, in the predominantly Calvinistic Rockland community, certain to be seen as consistent with God's design for the enhancement of His glory and for the well–being of His people.

It must have been part of the conventional wisdom of right–thinking men and women of that day that the kinds of things Rockland farmers did, both in the normal course of duty and when engaged in their special, small efforts to secure an advantage, were useful, proper, and fruitful. Thus, by his activities, the hard–working, experimentally–minded farmer was thrice rewarded in whatever he endeavored to do. He improved his own position, he helped his neighbor, and he gained the respect of the small general public that constituted his association group.

For the man who was especially able and fortunate enough to own ample and fruitful land, the rustic Rockland world of 1800 was his to do with as he willed, so long as he defined his ambitions in its terms. He had the formal right to erect a mill on his land and to become a miller, if good fortune provided him with a suitable mill site. He needed no permit to build, no license to operate. If he were willing to apply himself energetically and efficiently he could be a farmer, a surveyor, a schoolteacher, and a lawyer; he could stand for public office, or he could be a preacher. And all at the same time, too, if he were so inclined. There was no one to ask him to set quotas, to demand he display his license, or to require he take advanced courses in preparation. His enterprise, rather than infringing on his neighbors and denying their cherished rights, served them through its capacity to increase their freedom, their possibilities, their range of action.

All that was asked of the Rockland farmer was that he be moderately successful in what he did and, further, that he not become a public charge. Thus, the natural economy of rural Rockland provided many opportunities for the ambitious individual to investigate and, if interested, to utilize to his own advantage. Given a mastery of productive techniques on the farm and a relative abundance of provision, the economic system rewarded exceptional activity richly. In this sense self–sufficiency and equality were encouraged, even within the dependency systems of the household–family–neighborhood.

As noted earlier Turner in his work maintained that individualism and an exuberant spirit characterized the frontiersman. For their part Elkins and McKitrick speak of the vast self–confidence men acquired at the frontier in Massachusetts.[13] Certainly, conditions like those prevalent in the rural back country of Rockland were in a similar sense conducive to the development of self–confidence in gifted, prosperous men. And this was true even as late as the 1830s. Simple decisions relating to the location of roads and docks changed the face of the countryside. The introduction of a crop new to the sector or of a new type of cottage manufacture could lead to the development of a productive and profitable branch of the general economy. And such introductions were within the power of very ordinary individuals. Important consequences were frequently observed to follow from quite inauspicious actions, benefiting both one's neighbors and one's self most of the time. It is not surprising, then, that in such an environment the successful realized from their experience a modest but entirely concrete sense of their own personal worth.

13. Elkins and McKitrick, "A Meaning for Turner's Frontier," *Political Science,* LXIX (1954), pp. 600-1.

5
BACK-COUNTRY SOCIETY

Rockland was never as free from the binding force of tradition as the frontier thesis would seem to imply. To some observers the back country had a distinctly conservative, tradition–protecting aspect. Dr. Green, for one, describes the Nyack neighborhood, prior to the founding of a village there, as a community composed of a few landholders who worked their farms and lived comfortably and happily within their means.[1] Others emphasized the insularity of the Rockland farmers and stressed the quaintness of their speech—a patois compounded of Dutch and English.[2] Often, to contemporary outsiders, the men and women of Rockland seemed typically Dutch rather than American and, accordingly, somewhat idiosyncratic. Writing in 1813, the gazetteer Horatio Gates underscored this impression when he said, "The honest simplicity of manners which characterize the Dutch population of the County is entitled to notice and to cordial commendation."[3]

1. Green, "Notes on Nyack §7," *Rockland County Journal,* April 13, 1878.
2. The colonial military records published in Cole, *History of Rockland,* contain numerous references to the qualities of the Rockland militiamen, emphasizing among other characteristics their limited knowledge of the English language and their backwardness. Cf. pp. 30-58, especially the letter of John Haring, dated March 28, 1776, pp. 32-3. Some impression of the backwardness in usage and style can be gained from reading a speech given by John DeNoyalles in 1774 in the Provincial Assembly. Cf. DeNoyalles, *Debates in Dividing Orange County.*
3. Gates, quoted in *Nyack Evening Journal,* May 10, 1889.

Throughout the agrarian period in Rockland the retention of Dutch traditions was promoted by the Dutch Reformed Church. One of the first acts of the settlers at Tappan had been to establish this church in October 1694. Until 1750 when a branch of the same denomination was organized at Clarkstown, the Tappan church was the only place of worship in Rockland. There the Dutch, Germans, Negroes, and Huguenots attended Sunday service; there they went to be married, to have their children baptized, and their dead eulogized.

During the colonial era this church performed many important functions for the local community. Its role was comprehensive rather than particular and included both sacred and secular elements. For eight years vital statistics for Orangetown were kept by the public reader of the church, who was one of the few literate individuals residing in Rockland at the time. The maintenance of other important records, such as those of weddings and christenings, remained the responsibility of the church throughout the period. The church also served as a clearinghouse for information relating to the needs and interests of the local people. When cattle strayed or property had been lost, or when plans for an approaching auction were being made, the farmers used the doors of the church as a bulletin board.

Its professional leader, the dominie, was always an educated outsider called by the membership to be their pastor under the aegis of the greater church. His task was to serve the community as guide and moderator. In addition to exercising moral leadership through his preaching, he arbitrated neighborhood disputes, dispensed advice when asked, and kept the congregation informed about current events. According to Green, a knowledgeable dominie was held in great esteem by his generally unlettered parishioners.[4]

With its multitude of useful functions and its strategic location in the social system, the church at Tappan was an important focal center of community life in back–country Rockland. Through his activities in and with the church, many a pioneer retained an identification with the Old World, thus keeping alive his sense of belonging within the compass of a cohesive cultural group. In fact, this identification was so substantial that the Tappan church continued services in the Dutch language as late as 1830, some 150 years after the first settlement. In this sense the Dutch Reformed Church acted as an

---

4. Green, *History of Rockland*, p. 139-40.

agency for the conservation of Old World traditions on the Rockland frontier. The cake of custom was not to be so readily broken as was implied in Turner's presentation of the frontier thesis.

Yet, not long after the initial settlement, an issue arose which revealed the fragility of the church's hold on its membership. In 1749, when a question arose as to whether the appropriate center of authority for the Dutch church was to be Amsterdam, Holland, or New York, the congregation at Tappan declared for New York and, in consequence, found itself at variance with its dominie, the Reverend Frederic Muzelius. To resolve the disagreement the congregation pensioned the dominie off and hired a replacement. Pastor Muzelius then set up another church, oriented towards Amsterdam, and sought to bring the flock back into the fold. According to Reverend David Cole, however, "The body of the congregation—a few only were with Muzelius—was with the uprising for Americanization."[5]

This disagreement was no isolated event. It was only the first of a number of similar conflicts in Rockland. During the early nineteenth century the Tappan church endured numerous schisms. One such incident, leading to the organization of an entirely new congregation, occurred in the Greenbush neighborhood in 1812. It gives some impression of the governing issues in these schisms. According to the account in Cole's *History of the Reformed Church of Tappan, New York,* the Greenbush people were interested in education and in the teaching of English. Asserting itself, the neighborhood applied to Dominie Lansing, then pastor at Tappan, for permission to organize a new Reformed Church. Among the reasons offered was the distance from the Tappan church—approximately three miles—as well as the desire for English preaching. Permission was refused. Nevertheless, the petitioners persisted. After an application to the governing body of the general area, which also refused permission, the Greenbush insurgents took their case to a different denomination, and in October of 1812 they organized as a Presbyterian Church. Of the ten charter members of the new congregation, nine were Blauvelts, that is, Dutch in their ethnic origins and descendants of old Rockland. Their common progenitor had come to the county over one hundred years earlier as a Tappan Patentee and was one of the founders of the Reformed Church at Tappan.

5. Cole, *History of the Reformed Church,* p. 25-46; also *History of the Classis,* pp. 227-9.

The hegemony of Dutch Calvinism continued to disintegrate between 1790 and 1830. In addition to the recurrent schisms which disrupted the established congregations, new doctrines appeared and attracted the interest of the farmers. Baptist and Methodist preachers, who arrived on the county scene almost simultaneously, carried their ideas about salvation and commitment into the rural households. Encouraged by their preaching, personal inspiration and the struggling conscience came to replace the establishment institution on the rural scene. According to Dr. Green, whose description of the role of the Dutch church we have been following to a large extent, these doctrines represented a democratizing movement and a sharp break with the Old–Country tradition.[6]

Nicholas Gesner, our farmer from the preceding chapter, was one of those who cast his lot with the new inspiration. A committed Methodist, he testifies in his Diary to the strong and special feeling that accompanied religious fellowship at the meetings he attended.

> The Greatest Sermon perhaps ever preached at Rockland on the Slote was preached at New Landing [today's Piermont] School house this night by Tho. T. Witsel . . . The School house was completely filled with hearers. He Witsel in his introduction touched on the Roman Catholic Church Despotism and power. His text was 62 Chapter Isaiah 10 Verse; a Wonderful Sermon. He pointed the obstruction in the Way of Zion in various ways, the Storms, after many things, the Great Obstacle was Sectarian bigotry, faithfully in Christian love strived to Remove all prejudices, calling on Great and Small present Old and Young to assist in the Removal of their impediments. He was Wonderfully engaged. Closed with a most affecting exhortation.[7]

In the *History of Rockland County,* while discussing the democratizing movement encouraged by the new religious doctrines, *c.* 1880, Dr. Green concentrated on the Methodists. He attributed the expressive enthusiasm of this sect to the youth of the teachings and the extent to which these teachings stressed a direct relationship between the individual and God. Green then went on to maintain that in Methodism each individual was a "personal and special factor in the care of divine providence."

On the other hand, in Methodism, just being was never sufficient. This private relationship with God demanded an active commitment on the individual's part. "By the teaching that without constant re-

6. Green, *Op. Cit.,* p. 249.
7. Gesner, *Diary,* October 17, 1832.

ligious struggle he will fall from grace," Green continues, "his religious life becomes a fervid effort to remain steadfast in the faith." The association of individuals equal before God, working together for common ends, is also important. "By the government of his church," Green writes, "he is placed in contact with others as earnest as himself, and in the class meetings, a form of open religious confessional, the prayer meeting, and the love feast, encouraged and strengthened by religious association, his enthusiasm becomes more intense." While the activity described involves association, the focus continues on the individual, his personal engagement, and his self–realization. In essence, with the coming of the new doctrine, one was free to stand with God, or to sink into iniquity. Duty was defined in personal terms and demanded an active commitment to self–realization.

Contrast this new faith with the old way in Rockland. Early in the settlement period the Dutch Reformed Church at Tappan had maintained a virtual monopoly in moral authority. This church was a cloak and a comforter. It was also an important locus of social interaction. By means of its persuasive power and its strategic location, it served as a vehicle for the perpetuation of status distinctions and the retention of certain Old–Country folkways. Newcomers to the country often assented to its authority and adopted it as their church. It seemed the proper thing to do, for at a superficial glance its favors seemed important and its sway unassailable. To this extent, then, the religion of the Dutch church insulated the Rockland pioneers against the disintegrating influence of the frontier environment and was, consequently, tradition–conserving.

But the Tappan church, which might have given substance to concepts of propriety and collective responsibility, turned out to be only mildly effective as a conserving force. In the face of pressures generated by the consuming, disruptive, secular experience that characterized rural Rockland, it reluctantly gave way and eventually lost its hold on the Rockland public. Time and again groups from within the congregation broke away and erected new churches, Presbyterian as well as Reformed. As a result, the traditions the establishment church had reinforced, while apparently important, atrophied.

With the turn into the nineteenth century, innovative doctrines penetrated into the county and added intensity to the democratizing movement within religion. These new doctrines dignified the common-place activities necessary for existence on the farms. Unique forms of justification and interaction developed in conjunction with them and, in time, came to be accepted as traditional in their own right. These forms, when featured as Methodism, were expressly conducive to encouraging self–reliance, elation, and a sense of communion with one's fellows while simultaneously demanding upright action as the price of grace. Such action, although private in its core, was often carried on in association with one's fellow communicants.

We find then a shift in doctrines from an establishment religion to one consonant with concrete experience in America. Eighteenth–century Rockland was, above all, a place where men and women had to work hard just to keep the wilderness from their gardens. They also had to be prepared to undertake tasks for which they had re-ceived little or no prior training, and were frequently very much on their own. Rockland was also a place where singular acts of initiative carried with them long–term consequences. An extraordinary amount of special decision–making was demanded of the pioneers. Uncer-tainty was an integral part of life and the routines which did exist were *ad hoc* constructions taken from alien systems and combined with on–the–spot innovations.

In the first days simple questions such as what crop to plant and how best to till the land had not been answered and were open to judgment and doubt. A calendar designed for European purposes needed adaptation to the natural rhythms of Rockland experience. The fair division of property, the location of a road which was to carry its burden for centuries, what to do about poison ivy, and the need for a new gristmill were all subject to individual option. In such a place, the religion which was most appropriate was the one that chal-lenged its adherents to prove their worth. And it was just such re-ligions, stressing a personal relationship between active individuals and possible grace, that eventually came to play an important role in the Rockland countryside.

This special decision–making and the uncertainty it entailed were the epitome of the existential frontier as defined heuristically. They are also essential to our understanding of life in pioneer Rock-land altogether, not only of its religions. They interpenetrated the countryside and left their mark on every relationship. Doubt was a constant companion of all economic activity, and it was absolutely essential to be alert in even the simplest transactions. Nicholas Gesner, for example, tells of some woolen cloth which had been returned to him by a fuller after processing. Following a somewhat tortured calculation as to the amount he had expected returned, Gesner comments, "It appears each pound (of yarn) had given one yard fulled— wove very thin." According to Gracie, his wife, to whose judgment he deferred in this matter, the fuller should have returned them five ells (over three yards) for each pound of yarn. In another instance Gesner went to great lengths to calculate the quantity of grain sent to the miller, John Nagle, and the flour returned by him. He examined results for a period of one month and then commented, "I think Nagle an honest miller. The reason of trying this experiment is, I having a good opinion of J. Nagle, in order to see if there would be as great lack here as with others whom I have heretofore tryed."[8] Gesner ends his comment at this point, however, and we shall never know whether Nagle was as honest a miller as Gesner assumed.

Whenever Gesner hired people to perform special services he would carefully analyze the results obtained, recalculating inputs and outputs, and comparing expectations with actual results. The absence of established norms and standardized items purveyed at set prices made such close calculation and careful evaluation a necessity, and a certain prudence in practical matters accompanied and tempered the farmer's approach. It is interesting to note that this pervading uncertainty in practical affairs also had its parallel in the new religions, in the constant fear of a personal fall from grace.

Such as it was, government, too, made its demands on individuals. It was a thing of bits and pieces, and most often was a direct product of local enterprise. Coping with an unorganized environment, citizens had put together a makeshift government designed for the transaction of public business. True, in organizing matters they had followed forms specified by the provincial and state governments, but the prevailing style was voluntaristic. There were no qualified administrators nor was there any planning in terms of objectives and efficiency. Instead, fellow citizens, elected by their peers, arranged to get things done as best they could. Everyone who was capable was expected to serve his time in office at some point, and

8. *Ibid.,* January 5, 1833.

such administration as there was consisted of a set of limited, direct operations carried on, for better or for worse, by the current incumbents. In 1800, for example, there were 42 political offices to be filled in Orangetown. At that date the census reported 310 male residents in the town over the age of sixteen. The offices to be filled included a Town Clerk, a County Supervisor, Assessors, a Collector of Taxes, a Justice, and three Constables to keep the peace. In addition, there were two Overseers of the Poor, several Fence Viewers, a Pound Master, five School Commissioners, and nineteen Overseers of the Highways. No individual, of course, was expected to earn his living from the office he held, and officials were generally chosen from among property holders. They worked sporadically and were paid on a *per diem* basis for what they did in service to the town.[9]

When something requiring public funds and public cooperation needed doing, in most cases whoever stood to gain the greatest advantage did the work. Self–interest was the primary force impelling projects towards completion, and where individual advantage was absent or ill–defined, a project was likely to languish. In many instances an individual effort, however resourceful, was not sufficient, and if the potential beneficiary was to complete his project, he frequently found it necessary to explain to his neighbors the collective advantage to be found in that project. Given the deep seated suspicion prevailing, organizing people into a community effort was not always an easy task.

In such circumstances public leadership was a constant test of competence. Ultimate decisions as to the appropriate outlay of public funds and the coordination of cooperative efforts remained in the hands of the constituency. Yet, commonly, the actual performance of a public act was dependent on the initiating individual and on the associations he could generate. The scene of activity was always close at hand and through direct observation the electors had opportunities to familiarize themselves with the accomplishments and to test the capabilities of the officeholder. According to John J. Haring in *Floating Chips*, "Economy in public expenditure was considered an old time virtue to be commended, and extravagant outlays a vice

9. Budke, *Historical Manuscripts,* vol. E. Among the manuscripts is an act for the relief of the poor in Orange County, dated December 31, 1768, providing that the freeholders allot £10 for the poor and 8 shillings a day to the Clerk for poor work. See also *Original Records of Orangetown,* 1765-1819 (Budke Collection, New York Public Library).

to be sternly discouraged and rebuked." Public accountability was mandatory and terms of office were short. In sum, a high level of performance was expected of those elected to the service of their neighborhoods, and any individual who aspired to bring about a presumed improvement was watched closely. Again, the prevailing ethos offered a set of values and a structure of relationships congenial to a voluntaristic society by providing direct rewards for effort and engagement and, when warranted, sanctions in the form of an objective fall from grace—this time in the eyes of one's fellows, should one be found in fault.

The product of a few years at a backwoods school, the Rockland farmer was expected to perform complex economic, political, and religious tasks intelligently. While generally he had kinfolk and neighbors to whom he could turn for advice and assistance, those close to him were usually little better equipped than he himself to cope with the manifold problems of daily existence.

In addition to the private activities necessary for the homestead's continued well–being, the farmer–freeholder was expected to do his neighborly duty, especially where he was more literate than most—but always in his own inimitable fashion, of course, for the obligatory act pertained to his unique capacities. He might be asked to assess his neighbor's property or to adjudicate disputes. His informed opinion in any special area, such as Gesner's with respect to boatbuilding, was a public resource. Militia duty, public office, and schoolteaching all had claims on him. Were he a forceful, devout individual, his congregation was certain to makes its demands on his time and skill. When his place was conveniently located, his neighbors assumed he would keep store for them. All in all, then, here was a situation in which a heavy burden in terms of expectations lay on the head of each and every capable member of the community.

Singular circumstances called forth a stream of immediate judgments from the participating individuals. The web of daily experience was drawn out in tension between active commitment and the fear of overstepping. Undeniably, the agrarian society in Rockland provided many opportunities for advantage and independence. But there were also costs. The personal load of work that each man and woman carried was heavy and demanding. Much of it was arduous physical labor; in addition, frontier circumstances obviated the routines and conventions that make things easier in a more hierarchical society.

Thus the "free" man was fastened down to the details of his particular acts. The householders, living down the road from each other, spent much of their day in relative solitude, or, when grouping, with their nearby kin–neighbors. Except for the occasional country peddler or circuit preacher, the stranger from beyond the neighborhood was a rarity. Yet, if Gesner's *Diary* is correct, a real respect for speculation and thoughtful examination prevailed, one which manifested itself in a rich religious experience. For example he wrote in his diary in 1832:

> I & Herbt Lawrence Argument on the way of salvation. It appears he supported the idea that what Christ had suffered on the Cross was nothing to man's salvation. That Christ was only a Man, possessing more of the Divine nature than any other man, that Christ was only an example to us . . . etc.

Green also underlines the extent to which education was esteemed —for good reason, too, because literacy was a form of personal power.

Nevertheless, the homesteaders were consistent with their way of life, and reflected in their attitudes their commonplace experience. Absorbed in material tasks, they dealt with ideas much as they did with their possessions, and whatever fancies they had were pragmatic. Their schools were simple in plan and organized with the object of developing in the students the skills necessary for the completion of immediate tasks. As we have seen already, when their religious expression had developed in its fullness, it provided an ideological base for their practical efforts. It was something very much like themselves, for it was ungainly, exciting, artless, and preoccupied with uncertainty.

A situation so demanding must have been especially difficult for inept individuals. Everyone could not have been so talented that circumstances bent easily to his will. With vigor at a premium and independence in thought and action profitable, those who were dependent or incompetent certainly were at a disadvantage to their more self–reliant neighbors. It would not be surprising to discover that frustration and apathy characterized many of the farm folk. For, with interpersonal competition a standard element in most relationships, and wariness functional, those who found the situation especially trying would certainly respond defensively or withdraw completely.

While information about those to whom back–country life had turned out to be particularly aggravating or oppressive is at best fragmentary, disagreements are known to have taken place in the neighborhoods. A survey by George Budke of extant bail bonds originating in Rockland prior to 1800, which he has included in his *Historical Manuscripts,* indicates that trespass and default were common causes for civil action. Frequently, the parties to these actions were respectable freeholding farmers who lived on adjacent plots. Undoubtedly, the vagueness with which boundaries had been drawn during the settlement period contributed to these conflicts, as did the absence of precise standards in exchange transactions.

Reported criminal actions emphasized bastardy proceedings. In this regard Budke writes, "In reading early court records of Rockland County, one is driven to the conclusion that illegitimate births were of not infrequent occurrence."[10] He then goes on to point out that the Overseers of the Poor spent a great part of their time bringing reluctant men to court as a means of forcing them to support the children they had fathered. Every effort was made to avoid situations in which dependent children would become charges of the community, for the cost of their upkeep came out of the pockets of the citizenry, and therefore was seen as an infringement on the individual's right to spend his own money as he saw fit. Where a person did become dependent, a common practice was for the town to auction his services off to freeholders on an annual basis, these freeholders to provide for the keep of the person as part of the compensation agreement. In this manner the town resisted the development of an administration for managing welfare problems.

More significant, however, are strong indications that some of the hostility incidental to the prevailing ethos was socialized and displaced—that is, directed outward against the Negro residents of the county. Black men and women comprised some ten percent of the Rockland population in 1800 and were at that time a major part of the non–property–holding labor force. A convenient pariah class, of whom nine–tenths were slaves, they were especially vulnerable to official enforcement, and Budke in his notes to his abstracts of the

10. Budke, *Extracts on the Early Court Records of Rockland County,* with notes on the same, p. 3 (Budke Collection, New York Public Library).

early court records of Rockland County observes, "The relatively large number of Negro offenders against the laws in the early days is noticeable." In the same work he also points to the severity with which punishment was meted out by local authorities. Floggings were frequent and banishment from the county was not uncommon.

In the competitive milieu of Rockland, where personal assertion and righteousness were significant components of the ascendant personality type, instances of conflict among individuals and of standardized techniques for displacing hostility are to be expected. What is more important for this analysis, however, is a consideration of factors and techniques which intervened to mitigate discord and to maintain, at a reasonable cost, the peace and prosperity of the community. How was it possible for this society of individuals to maintain some semblance of harmony in their interpersonal relations while, figuratively, they were climbing all over each other?

For one thing, the setting itself operated to dampen conflict. The very isolation which signified the frontier style of life for Paxson, was enforced by geography on the Rockland farmers. As a result they had little opportunity for social interaction. As we have previously indicated, houses were located at separate farms, a third to a quarter of a mile from each other, and the paths connecting these farms were generally poor. Only a few public highways were regularly worked.

To cite one example, the wagon road nearest the Nyack neighborhood was the King's Highway. It ran along the west slope of the Palisades from Tappan north to Haverstraw, hugging the sidehills, meandering here and there to avoid the quaggy swamps that lay in the path of a more direct route. To get to this road a Nyack resident had to climb some two miles across the Palisades, making his way along the private lanes the various farmers had cleared for their own convenience. Such lanes were the primary means of interfarm communication in the county.

No special rights of way existed, and passage along the trails was obstructed from time to time by the gates which each farmer constructed to mark the boundaries of his farm. Propriety required that these gates be kept closed at all times, and the traveler who passed through them was expected to secure them after his passage. As these farm–to–farm lanes had never been designed for heavy loads and were generally ill kept, if kept at all, the only practical means of transport for the traveler was on horseback or by foot. In the spring, when the heavy rains washed the farmers' lanes off the sides of the hills, and the lanes close by the lowland bogs disappeared altogether, travel was especially difficult. Such roads, of course, discouraged aimless socialization and in degree, restricted the farmer and his family to the immediate neighborhood.

Their life was not entirely solitary, however. While the daily round confined them, there were, from time to time, occasions of a different order that offered relief from the prevailing isolation. Such occasions provided for extensive social interaction, were distinctly dionysiac in flavor, and counterbalanced the loneliness and insularity. Huskings, weddings, and political conventions were such occasions. According to Dr. Green, everyone in the county attended wedding parties. Drinking and dancing on the barn floor, horse racing, and wrestling were all parts of the celebration. In his notebook J. E. Sickels describes a similar occasion—the General Training which took place annually in a field on the north side of Middletown Road near today's Pearl River. "It was a kind of mustering of the yeomen and others round about the neighboring country, to take part in military drills," he writes. "It was generally observed as a holiday, and horse racing, dancing and other sports and entertainments were indulged by the people."[11]

Assemblies were also a mechanism for organizing religious expression, especially among the Methodists. They served to integrate the individual expression of the spirit into a common kinship under God. Camp, class, and prayer meetings drew together the independent souls into a conclave for mutual expression. Great crowds, sometimes as large as three thousand or more, seeking their God and His grace were attracted to these assemblies. Again and again Nicholas Gesner describes such meetings as exciting and fulfilling, with evocative preaching and tears, with song and with many a bowed knee. "Oh! Glorious work of God!" he exclaims.

In its own special way the assembly tapped the sources of unity within the community. Much that was worthwhile emerged from the excitement generated. Independent in spirit, untrained in and unused to social graces, buoyant, and with energy in abundance, the participants celebrated in a manner consistent with their total outlook. Their

11. Green, *History of Rockland*, pp. 37-8, and Sickels, *Notebook*, p. 155, Item §747.

moments of togetherness were short while their appetites were long. Good manners and propriety were probably not their strong points, and their enthusiasm sometimes got the better of them. But underneath the pandemonium there was usually a serious effort, and one that worked for the benefit of the community. Someone got married, or was nominated, or trained for his militia duties. Some measure of unity was organized out of the many possibilities for disagreement. And at the camp meetings of the co–religionists, there were even some who, after wrestling for a period with the devil, felt themselves saved. "Oh! Glorious work of God!"

Furthermore, the assembly had another practical purpose—it served as a personal purge. It provided an opportunity for lonely people to shout out some of the stored up bile left over from the winter. The wrestling and tippling, the cheering and singing and crying offered the back–country people a sharp contrast to the mundane duties that crowded every day. And after the occasion had subsided they were left with something to mull over and talk about. The assembly thereby provided a catharsis for whatever personal torment the isolation incident to frontier–type existence generated.

During the rural–settlement period Rockland was a testing ground. Opportunities abounded and frontier ways of acting, as described earlier, were encouraged. Today's savings sponsored tomorrow's prosperity, and often paid an immediate return as well. Even an element of philanthropy was lodged in acts disrupting the established order, for improvements in the general welfare were frequently the result of projects directed towards a private advantage. Circumstances favored the person of talent and independence, and the land waxed fruitful as people directed their energies in limited but creative efforts.

At the same time an implicit contradiction was rooted in the back–country way of life, for competitiveness and distrust accompanied and compounded each instance of individual interaction. A gentle form of avarice prevailed and, given the wholehearted acceptance of personal initiative and progress, it might well have been the source of much misery and discord. Such would have been the case especially for individuals ill–matched in status or ability.

But circumstances often intervened to soften the impact of overbearing individuals. While progress was the style of the day, change came slowly in Rockland, somewhat more slowly than we would have expected from Turner's thesis. For one thing, remnants of a system of traditional authority which had been brought over from Europe helped make living possible in the new American habitat. Although diluted and disappearing, the Dutch ways helped sustain the weak and temper the strong. Scions of the old families dominated the township councils and intermittently resisted advance. A special patois supported a parochial outlook in the community and an establishment religion provided guidance. Thus, even while dying for want of nourishment, this transplanted European system helped ease the transition into the New World.

The environment itself, through its natural awkwardness, also managed to contain the progressive energies within civilized limits. Almost anything was possible, and rarely was it disallowed by anyone in authority. But, at best, that "almost" anything was difficult to organize. With people living at a distance from each other, most social interaction was confined to face–to–face relationships among neighbors, among whom expansion and improvement could generally proceed at a leisurely pace. Finally, what mass socialization existed was cathartic rather than contentious and served to stabilize relationships and support the cause of peace and harmony. By these various means, then, the rural society in Rockland, while steadily evolving into coherence with the material environment, managed to provide a modicum of ease for its less sure citizens. Potentially a steam kettle of a society, it operated at a very low pressure.

The unique quality of the rural society, however, was not to be found in its capacity to sustain the weak. Instead, it was the confidence and enthusiasm it built into so many of its people that counted and that reminds us most of the frontier paradigm. While the pace of progress in Rockland was slow its results were rewarding. Shaping the raw wilderness for productive purposes was never easy. Largely hand work, it took time, ingenuity, energy, and perseverance. Each stump, as it clung tenaciously to its personal share of the earth, symbolized the cranky, unwilling wild. The men and women who overcame that resistance and tamed that wilderness could hardly have emerged from their test of strength without a strong sense of their innate capability. In this great effort the free, the proud, the vigorous person had a distinct advantage over his less resourceful neighbor. The more emancipated the individual the greater were his or her chances. Through strength, through intelligence, and through the use of the exceptional in one's make–up, one accomplished—and in a way that was apparent to the others. In this manner, then, nature repaid with strong self–images the men and women who overcame the resistance she offered. They had reason to believe they had earned their pride.

In a simple, low–voltage way the back–country offered a situation where a measure of personal autonomy was both possible and profitable. Whether the men and women of agrarian Rockland were "new men" as de Crèvecœur had announced, we cannot tell. More likely, they expressed through their way of life a latent element of the human potential. What we can say with certainty, though, is that their situation favored self–sufficiency and that effort and industry, not position and birth, were to a large extent the foundation of their reward. Singular circumstances forced the farmers in Rockland to develop their own resourcefulness and, at the same time by keeping them apart, curbed tendencies to create discord. Isolation and social distance thus operated just as Paxson had suggested it might.

Custom's cake did not break, however; it crumbled. In Rockland, the old traditions simply withered away over time, yielding to a system of values more consistent with the prevailing material environment. Coincidentally, this new system grew elaborate in detail as the many individuals articulated its shape and substance in their transactions, their assemblies, their forms of worship. By 1800 the new system, woven with surviving elements of the old, had become accepted on its own terms as tradition also and was complete. As matter, the new system featured freeheld farms that were to a large extent self–sufficient. As ideology, the cornerstones of the new system were self–reliance and freedom, the values most cherished by the relatively equal freeholders who predominated in the county population and controlled its institutions. If this is what we mean by "frontier," then Rockland, as experience and process and place, was a frontier land throughout the eighteenth century.

Tunis Smith, one of these proud and energetic men, told us in his *Diary* that in 1810, at the age of 38, he left the old, rural way of life and moved to Nyack, to new encounters and undertakings. He did this in order to take advantage of the commerical opportunities the place provided and to promote improvements. Let us now follow him there.

6
THE FOUNDING OF THE VILLAGE

Adrian Lammerts (meaning Adrian, Lambert's son), originally of Tiel, Holland, was a leader in the group of pioneers that purchased land at Tappan in the late seventeenth century. Sometime around 1684 he removed to Rockland and there, near the green bush that marked the north boundary of the Tappan Patented lands, he built a homestead and settled with his family. In time, that neighborhood came to be called first Greenbush then Blauvelt, following the construction of the Erie Railroad through the county a century later. According to family legend Adrian had been a blacksmith; hence, in the years that followed, most of his descendants took as their distinguishing patronymic the name Smith.

For four generations, descendants of Adrian Lammerts, the smith, lived quiet lives on the rural homesteads at Greenbush. One was a miller, another a weaver, and a third, a surveyor. All were farmers. Generally they were prosperous and most of them owned slaves. The Smith family was prolific of sons, and a number on gaining manhood moved elsewhere to seek their fortune. The father of Gerrit Smith, the famous New York abolitionist, was one of these. Others, however, remained close to the family farm and worked the soil as their fathers had done before them. Among these was Isaac P. Smith, the father of the Tunis Smith whose diary we paraphrased earlier. A great–grandson of Adrian's, he seems to have spent most

71

of his life operating the farm at Greenbush. He was among the more prosperous men of Orangetown, and in 1796 the assessor ranked him fifteenth from the top in the value of his holdings out of 142 property owners reporting. He was also, according to one source, an "old tory" in politics.[1]

In 1810, Isaac's oldest son, Tunis, put his part of the family farm out to shares and moved to Nyack, settling on a plot close by the river landing, which he had acquired through his wife's family. Shortly afterwards his brother Peter sold his share in the Greenbush homestead and followed Tunis to Nyack. There, after relocating near the landing place, the two brothers became actively engaged in commerce.

Despite the extensive sandstone quarrying along the Hudson River at the time, the Nyack neighborhood was still very rural when the Smiths moved there. Only seven houses were within the limits of what is today the incorporated village of Nyack, and only twenty–two households were located in the area stretching from the Clarkstown line to the point where today's Thruway enters Rockland.[2] Abram Tallman operated a store at the landing. Otherwise, there was little to indicate that the neighborhood was on the verge of a vigorous expansion. Such development as was underway was concentrated in today's Upper Nyack, at the point where the road leading across the Palisades and into the center of the county began. (See Map IV.)

An incident of progress had combined with the accidents of geography to attract the Smiths to the river landing at Nyack. The transforming agency was not local; instead it was situated far to the west, at the point of Rockland where the Ramapo River cuts its pass through the mountains. There, early in the colonial period, iron ore had been discovered in workable quantities, and in time mining and smelting had developed. In the springtime of hope, ambition overstepped itself and operations in the Ramapo area were carried on in a grandiose manner. Failure followed almost immediately, however, and an international scandal developed. Later, following the Revolu-

---

1. *Orangetown Tax List for the Year, 1796.* Computations are the author's. Also, interview with Lawrence W. Coates, 1914, by J. Elmer Christie, notes of which are on file, Nyack Library.
2. The limits of the present incorporated village of Nyack enclose an area of approximately ⅔ of a square mile. The larger area mentioned comprises some 3 square miles. See also, Budke & Christie, *Old Nyack.* In 1810, 119 persons, eight of whom were slaves, resided in the Nyack neighborhood. Over half of that number was in what is today South Nyack. *Manuscripts of Census, 1810, Rockland County, N.Y.*

tion when the actual limitations of the site had become apparent, the mines and furnaces reopened but continued operations on a much reduced scale.[3]

When considered in terms of early industrial techniques, the site had many advantages, and by 1800 several individuals were engaged in manufacturing along the Ramapo, most notably, the nail–makers J. G. Pierson and Brothers. The Piersons had been attracted by the abundant supplies of hardwood available and the ready access to water power. A further inducement was a friendly loan of $5000 from the State of New York which enabled them to move their operations from Wilmington, Delaware. By 1815 industrial output in the Ramapo valley had grown to a considerable figure for the time and place. The Piersons alone, for example, had drawn a work force of 150 to their factory site and produced 500 tons of cut nails that year. Abram Dater, an ironmonger who was situated a short distance up the pass, reported in 1813 that he operated six forges and employed some 140 persons. And in 1815, Jacob Sloat built a three–story factory near his father's tavern for the manufacture of cotton cloth.[4]

While the Ramapo manufacturers undoubtedly benefited greatly from the rich resources available in the heavily wooded mountain valley, they were at the same time very much its pioneers. For example, the Piersons required a special iron, imported from Russia, for their operations and were unable to use the local product. As a result their freight problems were doubly difficult. As we have stressed earlier, no direct, commercially practical roads existed in Rockland during the early decades of the nineteenth century. The nearest natural route suitable for heavy freight, the Hudson River, lay on the opposite side of the county at a considerable distance from the Ramapo factories. To reach the river from their remote position the manufacturers were compelled to cart goods for many miles over the crude back–country roads by horse– or ox–drawn wagon.

At that date two alternative freight routes were in general use. One, a road some sixteen miles long, linked the Ramapo workshops to the river landing at Haverstraw in Rockland County. Traversing

3. For details, see Ransom, *Vanishing Ironworks,* esp. pages 17-52, Hewitt, *Ringwood Manor,* pp. 1-11, and Hasenclever, *Peter Hasenclever.*
4. Sloat was a third generation Rocklander of Dutch extraction. His father, Isaac, was tavernkeeper at the Orange Turnpike way station which came to be called Sloatsburg, and was one of the more prominent men in the county. Abram Dater was a New Jersey man of unknown extraction.

rough country, it bore north away from the main line of trade. The other route was the Orange Turnpike which linked New York with Albany. From Ramapo it ran south through New Jersey, a land distance of 32 miles, and met the Hudson at Hoboken. Neither of these routes was entirely satisfactory and, obviously, it was in the interest of the Ramapo men to devise improved means which would offer shorter, smoother, and more direct routes to the Hudson. (See Map III)

It was in this impulse that the Ramapo manufacturers found common cause with Tunis and Peter Smith of the Nyack neighborhood. Some of the Ramapo men favored improving the existing Haverstraw road, but others, notably J. H. Pierson, desired construction of a Nyack–Ramapo turnpike. These latter contended that the Nyack road would shorten the overland distance to the river by five miles and, further, that the Nyack landing, relatively deep at the shore side, was less likely to freeze over in winter than were the shallow alternatives, Haverstraw and Piermont.[5] The chief obstacle to this route was a deep swamp at Greenbush. Considerable upkeep was anticipated if through passage was to be maintained. As early as 1806, Pierson called attention to the advantages of a Ramapo–Nyack connection, and shortly afterwards set about marshaling support among favorably disposed Rockland easterners for a Nyack turnpike corporation. At about the same time Tunis Smith began purchasing land and water rights at the Nyack landing.

Many of the back–country farmers did not approve of efforts to further the economic integration of the county. Through their influence in local government, attempts to appropriate public funds for the construction of roads and bridges suited to the needs of the Ramapo manufacturers received short shrift. These farmers maintained that such projects constituted an invasion of their rights. Others, however, saw the road and bridge projects in a different light. These men too had been bred in the back–country society, but they recognized opportunity in opening the land to improvements, rather than in securing it in isolation against alien influences. They were the men who established stores at the riverside, or built docks, or subdivided their farms for development.

---

5. Cf. Letter of Pierson in Cole, *op. cit.*, p. 269 *ff.*, also Pierson, "Letters Written in 1826," *Rockland Record*, 3, (1940), pp. 83-6.

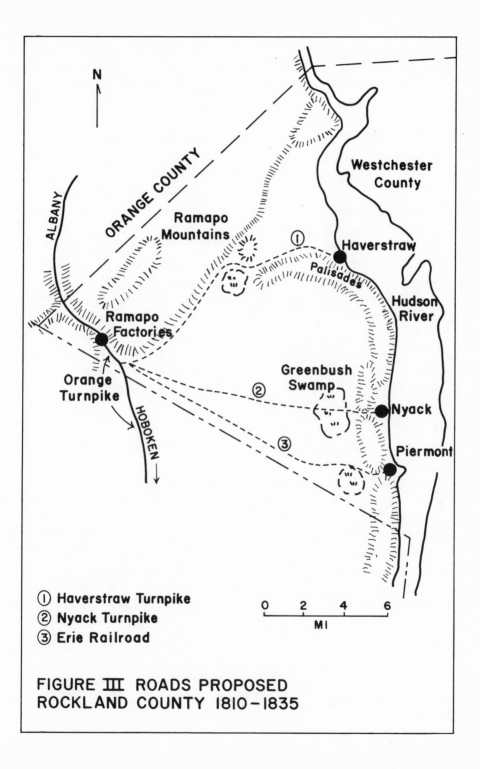

N

ALBANY

ORANGE COUNTY

Westchester County

Ramapo Mountains

① Haverstraw

Palisades

Ramapo Factories

Hudson River

Orange Turnpike

HOBOKEN

Greenbush Swamp

② ③ Nyack

Piermont

① Haverstraw Turnpike
② Nyack Turnpike
③ Erie Railroad

0   2   4   6
MI

FIGURE III ROADS PROPOSED
ROCKLAND COUNTY 1810-1835

At that time roadbuilding projects had a distinctly private flavor. The state's role was to confirm rather than to execute, and before construction was possible, turnpike corporations sanctioned by legislative enactment and funded through public subscription had to be organized. The subscribers were to be compensated for their investment through the collection of tolls along the road.

To promote the turnpikes and to smooth the political path, the Ramapo manufacturers leagued themselves with those among the back–country men who stood to gain from road extensions to the river. As the landholders at the more convenient riverside locations were especially likely to be able to turn the road projects to their personal advantage, they received close attention from the Ramapo men. Concurrently, certain of the more alert back–country men had early seen the possibilities of such developments, and had moved to acquire property at the landing sites. In time a united front developed between the Ramapo men and these riverside entrepreneurs, and through their combined efforts authorization and capital for several improvements were obtained. A middling boom in turnpikes developed in Rockland, and among the roads that were built as a direct result of the boom was the Nyack Turnpike to Ramapo.

Two of the most active of those who saw in the turnpike boom an objective focus for their enterprise were Tunis and Peter Smith. Shortly after his arrival in Nyack in 1810, Tunis built a house for his family which he also opened as a store. Subsequently he constructed a dock at the riverside and a public road leading up from his new dock to his store. Today this road is Main Street in Nyack. Several years later when Peter also located in Nyack, he too opened a store in his house. Together the Smiths purchased a farm—the acreage of which comprised the center of today's village—and subdivided it into lots for real estate development. At the same time both were taking an active part in the campaign to secure legislative approval and funds for the construction of the Nyack–Ramapo Turnpike.[6] In one way or another the brothers Smith participated in just about every ambitious endeavor under way at Nyack during the first quarter of the century.

6. Budke, *Historical Manuscripts,* vol. E. See stock subscription list dated February 10, 1817, also letter from Pierson, and meeting notes for the years 1817 and 1818, all referring to the Nyack Turnpike. Budke Collection, New York Public Library.

And, in concert with their contemporaries, they literally transformed the substance of opportunity at the landing place.

The Smiths were not alone in enterprise at Nyack. From 1780 on, men had been attracted to the landing by the various opportunities it offered for exploitation. An early reason for moving there was the rich lode of sandstone outcroppings along the Hudson River bank; immediately following the Revolution, quarries were opened to the north and south of the landing. The brownstone from these quarries found a ready market in New York City, and they continued to produce stone profitably until 1840 when a better grade of stone came on the market. Subsequently, the quarries were abandoned and those who had cut stone in them drifted away.

Quarrying, in turn, had stimulated a demand for freight boats, and in answer to that demand, a boatbuilding and repairing industry developed along the waterfront. Others who made their homes at the landing were sailors on the river boats berthed there. To a great extent these activities were carried on in conjunction with the standard back–country farm pattern and many of the farmers' sons of the Nyack neighborhood began work as hands, or sometimes as captains, on their fathers' stone barges.

Expansion associated with stone quarrying and the attendant boatbuilding and freighting at Nyack lacked force, however, and was uneven in its impact. It did not result in the formation of a symbiotic community capable of maintaining itself in competition with other communities over the long term. This is consistent with experience elsewhere in Rockland at that date. Industrial ventures in the county during the early nineteenth century seem to have attracted a largely itinerant work force and thus rarely, if ever, brought about the development of permanent communities. Like the Haverstraw brickmakers and the Piermont roundhouse force later in the century, the quarry workers were transients, usually men alone. Few lived in settled circumstances and the crowded boardinghouse is a commonplace in the early census returns. Even the extensive operations in the Ramapo pass area did not draw a permanent work force there, and as manufacturing in that locality declined later in the century the working population moved on in search of new opportunities. In time, many of the factory sites there returned to the wilderness. By all indications, the situation was qualitatively different with commercial development. The people who gathered in response to its call engaged in a multitude of interrelated activities and formed village communities. The critical elements that account for the difference seem to have been the heterogeneity of the activities associated with commerce, interdependence, the fact that females had an important place, and the extent to which family relationships played a significant role in the total way of life.

The turnpike was completed eventually and came into general use around 1825. Its opening stimulated increased activity on all fronts at Nyack. The Smiths joined with their fellow storekeepers, John Green and Benjamin Blackledge, and the boatbuilder, Henry Gesner (nephew of Nicholas, the diarist), and built themselves a steamboat at Nyack for the New York trade. This boat, the first of many to be built at Nyack, was launched in 1827 and christened the *Orange*.[7] With her construction, another essential link between the productive back country and the burgeoning city was forged. Commanded by Peter Smith's son, Isaac, she soon captured a major portion of the river trade.

With the turnpike penetrating into the county and the *Orange* linking the Nyack landing with New York City, facilities for the handling of goods were marvellously improved. That this was the planned intention of the Nyack men is clear from the application they submitted to New York State requesting permission to lay out the Nyack Turnpike. Dated March 27, 1823, it states "that from the proximity of Nyack to the Emporium of the State, its landing, particularly during the winter season affords superior advantages and facilities for the transportation thence of all kinds of produce to New York markets." Taking advantage of these improvements, the back country farmers, who had been slowly recasting their productive efforts into market terms since the turn of the century, accelerated the shift from subsistance farming to cash crops. Shipping their produce by way of the turnpike and the *Orange*, they earned ready money which they spent to the advantage of the Nyack shopkeepers.

Eventually, this rural trade became the primary business of the place. Even after 1841, when the Erie Railroad connecting the com-

7. Cf. Green, "Notes on Nyack," *Rockland County Journal*, May 11, 1878, for a complete account of the construction and operation of the *Orange*. See also, Budke, *Historical Manuscripts*, vol. A, for the original of the subscription list of pledges for the *Orange*, dated March 17, 1825. According to this document the active parties in the enterprise were John Green, Tunis Smith, and Peter Smith.

peting river village of Piermont to the Ramapo workshops had been completed and the turnpike was displaced as a major outlet for manufactured products, Nyack still did not decline.[8] Instead, it took this loss of trade very much in stride and continued to expand. For by that date the hamlet which had grown up at the landing there had become the entrepôt for much of Rockland County. The combination of the turnpike, of stores and freight handling facilities at the nexus point, and of relatively fast passage to the city had proved very attractive, and the farmers had responded with increased business.

The traffic in produce also inspired the introduction of a variety of other ventures at Nyack. In 1827, Cornelius T. Smith, Tunis's son, built a hotel to provide accommodations for those who found it necessary to stay in the hamlet overnight. In 1832 Asiatic cholera appeared in New York City and those with the means to do so fled the city. As a result Smith's conveniently located hotel filled up with fugitives from the dread disease. They seem to have found benefits in their enforced stay for in the years that followed many returned to Nyack seeking a salubrious climate. By 1860 the village had established something of a name for itself as a summer boarding place for city residents.

William Perry took the lead in an entirely different line. In 1828 he opened a shop at his residence, employed several workmen, and began the manufacture of women's shoes in Nyack. Perry's business was far larger than his single shop would indicate, however, for it was the center of an extensive putting–out arrangement which he developed in cooperation with the farmers who came to Nyack to trade. He would provide them with leather and lasts on which they and their families could work during slow periods on the farm. He then purchased from them the finished goods they brought when they returned to the landing.

With the introduction of shoe manufacturing, boatbuilding and operating, hotel keeping, and farm–market merchandising, the essential features of Nyack's economic configuration–to–be had been set. The dispositions the brothers Smith and their fellow entrepreneurs

---

8. Another of Pierson's efforts to secure access to the river led to the construction of the Erie Railroad and to the development of the Tappan landing as the terminus for the road. The landing was renamed Piermont in honor of the enormous steamboat pier the railroad constructed there. Pierson's son-in-law, Eleazer Lord, was a prime mover in the venture and eventually took up residence at Piermont.

had made proved wise, and the landing place, which was "little more than unbroken forest," in 1800 had become a center of enterprise by 1835. The first dreams had materialized and new dreams had become possibilities.[9]

The individuals who had been the driving force behind these developments were very much of a piece with their back–country forebears. Their characteristic modes of action were in many ways similar to those which we earlier attributed to the pioneer at the frontier, and which we also found characteristic of the householders of rural Rockland. At Nyack these new pioneers encountered problems centering on the advance of business and a situation susceptible to change. Again, as had been true in the back country, mutual advantage followed from individual acts furthering self–interest. In most instances of progress there was little if any reliable information available from past experience. The individual who opened a store, laid out a road, or built a steamboat did so of his own volition, or in concert with equally independent individuals. He staked his future on his energy, his foresight, and his acumen. If alert, he seized opportunities as they appeared and worked both individually and in cooperation with others in the pursuit of practical ends. If there is a difference between the two milieus it is to be found in the degree to which village enterprise offered a large number of instances where a collective effort was necessary. The overriding spirit was voluntaristic, nevertheless, just as it had been in the back country earlier.

Isaac Smith provides an illustration of this pioneerlike process. Sixth in the line of descent from Adrian Lammerts of Tiel, Isaac was the oldest of Peter Smith's four sons. He was born on the Smith family farm at Greenbush in 1801 and came to Nyack with his parents while still a child. In his youth he was apprenticed to a local blacksmith who specialized in the fabrication of metal fittings for the boats under construction in the Nyack yards. Otherwise, his up-bringing and education had differed little from that of his paternal grandfather (whose namesake he was) some sixty years earlier.

Some two or three years after the steamboat *Orange* had been commissioned, Isaac was appointed her captain. It is difficult to ascertain whether he was properly qualified through experience or training

9. Wm. G. Haeselbarth, "A Backward Glance," *Rockland County Journal,* February 11, 1871.

for the assignment. As was frequently the case with Nyack young men of that day, he had probably skippered many a stone barge to the city. But steamboating was a new trade and the *Orange* was one of the first ships on the river. In any case, Isaac took command and for the remainder of his life he was known as a ship's master. With this designation, conventionally accepted, Isaac breaks in a small way with the past and embraces the new era of specialization. He becomes marginally, for the time is early and the new era has not yet hardened its grasp, an attribute of his trade, and to a certain extent his independence has been diminished. In assuming a specialized occupation, Isaac differs somewhat from his father and his uncle Tunis. Despite their many ventures into business, they always defined themselves, at least nominally, as capable in many trades and activities. Thus they retained the ambiguity which we discussed earlier under the rubric "jack–of–all–trades."[10]

Isaac's style was entirely consistent with the past, however. He was about thirty years old when he assumed command of the *Orange*. Riverboating on the Hudson in the 1830s was part business and part battle, and Smith was very much the man for both. In time each of the competing landing places had acquired a steamboat of its own and to test the mettle of their craft and to win glory for themselves, the several captains often raced their boats against each other. But the races also served to demonstrate the superiority of a particular boat, thereby bringing honor, and more importantly, business to its home landing place.

The rivalry between the three Rockland landings, Haverstraw, Nyack, and Piermont was especially intense. During races both crews and passengers became exceedingly partisan, and feelings often ran high. The fact that the *Orange* was the oldest of the steamboats and the least advanced technologically only added spice. Even though she was commonly regarded as something of a tub, the Nyack captain still was expected to excel in the competition. And he often did. When the *Rockland,* an opposition boat from Piermont, proved capable of outracing the *Orange* consistently, Captain Smith rose to the challenge. He fashioned a false bow for his boat and so increased her

10. The 1840 federal census includes a simple classification of occupations. Both Tunis and Peter Smith are identified therein as farmers. For the Nyack neighborhood, generally, out of 726 persons, 12 classify themselves in mining, 95 in agriculture, 15 in commerce, 107 in manufacturing, 26 in river navigation and 5 in the learned professions.

speed as to leave the opposition far behind.

But ingenuity and technical superiority were not the only means to excellence in riverboat competition. There were also other, more stirring moments, and Captain Smith made his mark in them, too. Writing in his diary in 1831, Nicholas Gesner tells of one such incident involving the *Orange*. According to Gesner the *Rockland* and the *Orange* tangled at the New York City dock. In their eagerness to make the landing first they crowded against each other and the *Orange* "jambed the *Rockland*'s yawl boat all to pieces."

Several years later Gesner returned again to the subject of riverboat competition and this time wrote in greater detail. A new boat out of Haverstraw, the *Warren*, had proved superior to the *Orange*. Not to be deterred, Smith built a new boat of his own, the *Arrow*, and challenged the supremacy of the *Warren*. In one instance of this competition observed by Gesner in 1837, the *Arrow*, with Captain Smith at the helm, ran on the *Warren* and rammed her amidships (or tried to; it is not clear which from the text). Gesner then continues, "Captain Isaac Smith of the *Arrow* pretended that the Captain of the *Warren* intended to crowd him on the shore, and that it was not the first time, and that he [Smith] was determined to show him [the Captain of the *Warren*] better." Gesner comments at this point in the narrative that some hotheaded men on board the *Arrow* wanted to run the *Warren* over, despite the fact that to do so would endanger the lives of some 200 persons. He then observes, in conclusion, that as an eyewitness he could swear that the *Warren* had not crowded the *Arrow* towards the shore and further, that he had spoken to Captain Smith about the matter!

Isaac Smith's achievements bulk large on the Nyack scene. The ships he built and captained carried the name of the village up and down the Hudson all the way from Albany to New York City. He was a strong man, fierce and determined. In keeping with family tradition he was loyal to his hamlet, a firm advocate of its improvement, and a leader in many of its endeavors. Throughout his active years he encouraged the expansion of boatbuilding at the landing, and in 1852 he threw his support and financial backing behind the construction of a foundry at Nyack for the manufacture of steamboat machinery.[11]

11. *Rockland County Journal*, January 1, 1853, also Green, "Notes on Nyack, §16" *Rockland County Journal*, June 15, 1878.

In 1860 Smith was a leader in the group seeking to organize a bank at Nyack to serve Rockland. He became its first president, and on the occasion of its opening was called upon to speak. Isaac Smith's few words, as reported in the October 16th edition of the *Journal,* were in keeping with the man—simple, direct, impatient, and practical. "You have called on me to make a speech, but that is not my trade," he declared. "If you had asked me to take the blacksmith's hammer and forge you a sword with which to —y (sic) some of the political parties who are making so much noise about our streets at night, I could have done that; or if you had given me a steamboat to manage, I could have done that too." Captain Smith then concluded by describing himself as one who had "rolled and tumbled about this little village" for fifty years.

Isaac Smith was coarse, and also he was strong. As had been true of his father and his uncle before him, he had a practical, inventive turn of mind. Quick to find expedients, he had a masterful grasp of material things. These, of course, are precisely the terms Turner used when he set out to characterize the frontiersman. They are, at the same time, substantially similar to those applied to Smith by his contemporaries. At the time of his death in 1869, the *Journal* declared in its eulogy, "None in this community [Nyack] has been more identified with its interests or done more to advance its prosperity, than the deceased. Identified with all its leading improvements, in those essential to our progress, he was a pioneer."

The various Smiths, and the others mentioned so far, are only those most readily identified as active in improvement in the village. Many others participated in developments there also. Throughout the second quarter of the century the hamlet at the landing place was growing rapidly and attracting venturesome people both from the back country of Rockland and from outside the county.[12] In each of these new people there was something of Adrian of Tiel, of Tunis, of Isaac Smith. Every store, every smithy, every carriage shop, and every shipyard in the growing hamlet was in its own way a challenge similar

12. In 1835, when it was still largely rural, Orangetown. had a population of 2,075. Only a few hundred of these people lived in the hamlets by the river landings. By 1855, the town contained two villages (Nyack and Piermont) which together supported a population of 3,662. Orangetown population for that year was 5,838, which means that the population of the remainder of the town was 2,176, indicating that it had increased only moderately over the period. See also Gordon, *Gazetteer of New York*, 1836, p. 658*f.* and French, *Historical and Statistical Gazetteer, 1860*, p. 569*f.* for contrast.

in essence to those that had confronted the pioneers on the advancing edge of civilization. Instead of problems referring to free land and boundaries, to the selection of crops and the clearing of the fields, or to dealing with the Indians, men found at Nyack, to use the terms Elkins and McKitrick employed when stating their claim for a second level of frontier experience, "a torrent of problems centering in the advance of business."[13] Potential gains and losses were larger, people had to cooperate more closely, and the competitive conflict was more intense at Nyack than it had been on the farms. But in the sense that problems and modes of coping persisted, that opportunities remained to be exploited, and that there were people seeking to promote the opportunities and to boost the village, life in Nyack retained distinctive characteristics associated with typical frontier existence.

During the period directly after the construction of the turnpike and extending through to midcentury, a crowd of boosters and enterprisers had gathered at the Nyack landing to reach out in all directions, probing the limits of possibility there. They took uncertainty in stride, and accepted self–interest and competition as a matter of course. They knew that the main chance lay with the continued growth of the village and that growth was dependent on many single acts of enterprise which always contained a gamble and expressed a private will. To succeed, it was necessary for the individual to gamble on the future Nyack offered, and thus test his strength and skill in competition with others.

Nevertheless, the Nyack entrepreneurs were also prudent men, and their deeds, while often unprecedented, were cautiously conceived. The first pride of the village, the steamboat *Orange,* was built with a view toward possible failure. Her planners took care when they designed her, Green reports, that if she should not succeed as a steamboat her engine could be removed and she could be converted into a coasting schooner. Furthermore, they did not neglect their culture, their children, or their community. They seem to have had something more than an economic organism in mind, and in seeking to perfect the place as an urban entity, they established several churches, founded a library, improved the school, and relocated the Post Office, mov-

13. Elkins and McKitrick, "A Meaning for Turner's Frontier," *Political Science.* LXIX (1954), pp. 339-41. See also, Paxson, *When the West is Gone,* p. 60 f., and Craven, "The Advance of Civilization into the Middle West in the Period of Settlement," in Fox, *Culture in Middle West,* p. 61.

ing it from the upper end of town to a site close to the landing place. Again, these are acts of a frontier way of life.[14]

These were the springtime days, when the sun shone on the venturesome and when faith in a better day tomorrow was often confirmed. Many of those who made up the crowd that had collected at the landing place over the half–century had been shaped in the back country where there had been much to encourage confidence and enthusiasm. They brought with them from there the pragmatism and independence that had characterized their fathers and grandfathers and had set it to work in a new milieu. They found at the river landing many opportunities for exploitation, and they engaged themselves with vigor as they set about effecting its transformation into an efficient and profitable entrepôt. And as the years wore on they were frequently richly rewarded for the chances they had taken.

14. Cf., Green, "Notes on Nyack, *Rockland County Journal, 1878;* also Budke & Christie, *Old Nyack.*

7
NYACK IN 1850

A thousand people, more or less, made their homes at the Nyack landing in 1850. They had settled together there during the quarter–century following the opening of the turnpike to Ramapo in 1826. Although Haverstraw and Piermont were both larger, Nyack was the most diversified in its interests. It was also charged with energy and full of enthusiasm and the place was on the move.

In that year William G. Haeselbarth, originally of Pennsylvania, established a newspaper at Nyack. In anticipation of the large role he hoped it would play in local affairs he named it the *Rockland County Journal*. The directors of the steamboat *Arrow,* Captain Isaac Smith, his brother David, and the storekeeper, D. D. Demarest, found their operations profitable and declared a dividend of eight percent at year's end. In response to the active trade that had developed at the landing place, Captain Smith had built a second steamboat for the New York run that year and christened her the *I. P. Smith* in honor of his grandfather. He equipped her with machinery manufactured at the steam foundry of William Crumbie & Son. Crumbie, a Scotsman, erected a foundry at the foot of Main Street during that summer of 1850. In the same year, Azariah Ross, a merchant who had kept store at Nyack a number of years earlier, built a workshop for the piano-maker James Thompson on Broadway, above Third Avenue. All in all, it was a busy year for Nyack, and her future looked bright.[1]

Nyack was still in the process of establishing its urban identity that year. The Federal Census for 1850, for example, listed twenty-eight men as farmers.[2] Thus agriculture remained one of the more important occupations in the neighborhood, exceeded only by ship carpenters, of whom there were 32 and shoemakers/cordwainers (29 in number). Other important categories were: boatmen (25), house carpenters (24), and laborers (16). Seven of the laborers were black, as were three boatmen. Nineteen persons in all are classified either as "Black" or "Mulatto" members of the labor force in the 1850 census. Altogether, 295 individuals are listed as employed in 53 different occupations. Their range is suggested by a sample of the terms used as designations: cooper, foundryman, gentleman, sash maker, pianoforte manufacturing, tinsmith, merchant, and painter—terms which reflect the emerging urban identity of the community. Except for one or two instances, only men were listed as employed in the 1850 census. Many young women carrying a family name different from that of the household head were listed with the several households and were probably servants. In subsequent censuses, "Servant" is an important category of employment.

A question on "value of real estate" was included in the 1850 census and, with reservations, we can use the findings to measure the relative economic status of individuals.[3] Some of the men listed as farmers have relatively large holdings in real estate and carry names indicating a Nyack lineage of long standing—Tallman, Lydecker, De Pew, or Cornelison. Others are entirely propertyless; most of these were black or foreign–born and were probably farm laborers. The remainder with large real estate holdings, defined as a value of $3,000 or above, were widows, landlords, gentlemen, and the sons of Tunis and Peter Smith. In all, 123 persons are listed in the census as owning real estate. Of these, sixty have holdings of less than $1,000. These individuals are not necessarily poor, however, since many who are later identified as movers and shapers of the urban way in Nyack reported relatively modest holdings in 1850. In fact, the wave of the future

1. *Rockland County Journal,* October 19, 1850, September 21, 1850, and January 4, 1851; also Green, "Notes on Nyack, §16" *Rockland County Journal,* June 15, 1878.
2. Throughout this chapter all statistical summaries and computations are the author's.

seems to have been decidedly undercapitalized there. Only one person primarily engaged in manufacture, the shoemaker William Perry, is included among those reporting more than $3,000. In sum, then, we find a relatively wide dispersal of small holdings among the commonplace storekeepers and the cottage manufacturers, and relative equality in terms of economic power. The large holdings, on the other hand, were concentrated in the hands of those who were identified with the old, back–country way of life. The brothers and cousins Smith, who amassed considerable wealth from their merchandising activities, of course constitute the prime exception to this general rule.

In 1850 Nyack's population was still substantially of local extraction; 919 of the 1,050 individuals making up statistical Nyack were listed as having been born in either New York or New Jersey.[4] Another 21 were born in other states of the Union, and only 110 were foreign–born. A table detailing birthplaces and occupation for the census of 1850 is shown below as Table I. Similar charts have been prepared for 1860 and 1870, and will be introduced sequentially in the next chapter, to be used for the identification of contrasts over time.

Table I: Birthplace/Occupation Profile. Nyack — 1850.

Birthplace	New York & New Jersey		Other US States		Foreign		Total	
Occupation	N	%	N	%	N	%	N	%
Agriculture	25	8.5	0	0.0	3	1.0	28	9.5
Ship Carpenters & Boatmen	57	19.3	0	0.0	3	1.0	60	20.3
Laborers & Service	12	4.1	0	0.0	4	1.4	16	5.5
Construction Trades	42	14.2	0	0.0	7	2.4	49	16.6
Shoe Manufacturing	27	9.2	1	0.3	1	0.3	29	9.8
Entrepôt Functions	90	30.5	7	2.4	16	5.4	113	38.3
Total	253	85.8	8	2.7	34	11.5	295	100.0

Source: Manuscripts of Census, 1850

3. Several people who are later known to be quite wealthy are recorded as having no real estate holdings in 1850, and for this reason it is questionable how much confidence should be placed in the recorded real estate holdings.
4. Throughout we have combined New York and New Jersey as birthplaces when we mean local in origin because social interaction across the border between Rockland and Bergen County, N.J. was common in the eighteenth and nineteenth centuries.

To give some meaning to "only," the term used above in reference to the number of foreign–born at Nyack, let us compare the situation there with that of its companion landing place village, Piermont. For the purpose of this and further comparisons we have drawn a sample from the census reports of Piermont. Piermont at the time was approximately twice as large as Nyack, but this sample is exactly the same size as the entire population of Nyack.[5] In Piermont, 420 of the 1,050 individuals in the statistical sample were foreign–born, and another 110 were born in states other than New York and New Jersey. Thus, over fifty per cent of the sample population was made up of "outsiders." Of the foreign–born, 383 came from Ireland. A larger number of person (358) reported themselves as employed in that village than had in Nyack (295), but in fewer lines of work (39 job categories in Piermont as against 53 in Nyack). Of the Piermont workers, 148 described themselves as laborers, and all but five in this category had been born in Ireland. The next largest employment group at Piermont were "Breakmen for the Erie Railroad." Of the 33 individuals so listed, 20 were born in Ireland. On the other hand, individuals having status positions with the railroad—superintendent, engineer, conductor, overseer, or fireman—were largely American–born. Of these 43 persons, 21 had been born in the New York/New Jersey area and another 19 in other states of the Union.

Piermont in 1850 was the eastern terminus of the Erie Railroad and was also the location of its major maintenance and repair shop. Railroading, a rapidly expanding industry at that time, attracted workers from many places. Despite the efforts of many local people to develop commerce there during the 1830s and '40s, it had not caught on. Instead the village remained a company town. The railroad dominated the situation, and the people who congregated at Piermont found it necessary to define their aspirations in terms of its intentions. By contrast, at Nyack, where the individuals were more likely to be autochthonous to the area, the crowd had collected together in response to opportunities that were polymorphic and indistinct. At Piermont initiative demanded that the individual define

5. As was the case for the statistical Nyack, the Piermont sample summarizes 25 consecutive pages of the census manuscript and includes 1,050 persons. The 25 pages begin with Orangetown household number 501 and continue through number 687. These particular pages were selected through an inspection of reported occupations by the author. *Manuscripts of Census, 1850 — Rockland County, New York.*

his objectives in terms complementary to the intentions of the railroad; at Nyack the definition of opportunity followed from individual acts of initiative.

If the comparison between villages contrasts different forms of an age to be, another comparison is also relevant. We can also ask how Nyack differed from the rural areas that had been left behind by progress. For that comparison we have again utilized a 25–page section of the 1850 census manuscript, this time the first 25 pages of the township returns from Clarkstown.

Clarkstown, in that year, was the most rural township in the county and politically the one most rooted in the past. The population was less alien in its origins than was Nyack's, but only marginally so. Of the 1,050 persons whose responses were reviewed, 76 were foreign–born, and six were born in states other than New York and New Jersey. The respective figures for Nyack were 110 and 21. The Clarkstown sample included more children and old people than that of Nyack (Table II). By all indications then, new people, especially young adults, had concentrated at the Nyack landing, while in the back country the population was more settled.

Table II: Comparison of Population by Age — Nyack/Clarkstown

	0-14 years	15-44 years	45 and over	Total
Nyack	369	530	151	1,050
Clarkstown	382	439	229	1,050

Source: Manuscripts of Census, 1850

The occupation list is much shorter for the Clarkstown neighborhood than for Nyack. Where the 295 Nyack workers had listed 53 different categories of employment, at Clarkstown the somewhat larger labor force (322) reported only 26 categories. One hundred and forty–five individuals at Clarkstown described themselves as farmers and another 74 as laborers. All but five of the farmers were born in the New York/New Jersey area, whereas 21 of the laborers were foreign–born. Of 53 laborers who were born locally, fourteen were black. Specialized occupations, which were few in number in Clarkstown, generally involved work in support of the farm economy —carpenters, basketmakers, merchants, and millers—although several reflecting the new era were also reported. These specialized occupations were exclusively the province of white, New York/New Jersey–born individuals.

Real estate holdings in Clarkstown were, on the average much larger than those of Nyack people (See Table III). This is as we would expect in a predominantly agricultural area. The Clarkstown lots were large and were operated as farms. There were very few of the small plots of limited value common to Nyack. Estimating from the extant evidence, it would seem that some 91 farms of workable size (defined as a value exceeding $1,000) supported a work force of some 219 individuals directly engaged on the farm. Thus more than two–thirds of the entire Clarkstown labor force was so employed.

Table III: Real Estate Holdings Reported, 1850, for Nyack and Clarkstown

Holdings ($)	0-999	1-2,999	3-7,999	7-22,000	Total
Nyack	60	40	12	11	123
Clarkstown	5	18	47	15	96

Source: Manuscripts of Census, 1850

What we find in the rural area then is a labor force largely devoted to farming and relatively undifferentiated as to specialization. This stability existed despite the shift from subsistence to cash crops which had been going on for over a half–century. Except for people new to the area and those habitually low in status, such as the black workers, the distribution of wealth in the neighborhood was still relatively even. Consequently, the salient features of our earlier description of the back country continued to endure in Clarkstown. Independent individuals operated farms they held in fee simple, and it is likely that they found it necessary to perform a variety of tasks as part of their daily routine. By comparison with this homogeneous activity, Nyack, in 1850, had already begun to show evidence of its urban–industrial identification, with job specialization and economic class distinctions emerging as pertinent characteristics of the landing place environment.

Trade and traffic between the back–country farms and the metropolitan center at New York City continued to be the prime business of Nyack in 1850. The county was flourishing, with cottage artisans and produce farmers everywhere. The steamboat line operated by the brothers Smith afforded rapid and convenient access to the city. The line also had docking facilities and a general store at Nyack. Several other enterprising townsmen had established stores and shops in the village; some were general purpose, while others offered specialties. At the same time, entirely different businesses were appearing on the local scene, such as the pianomaking establishment mentioned earlier and a cedar pail factory. In those years Nyack's advantage lay in its excellent commercial location and its rapidly increasing population.

At the water's edge several ship carpentry firms had established yards and had built ways for the construction of boats for the coasting trade. Conventionally, these firms had a somewhat ephemeral existence, coming together for a job or two, or maybe for a season, and then dissolving after they had completed contracted work. Several of the builders had acquired a reputation as "boss carpenters" and headed such firms as there were. In October, 1850, the partners William Dickey and James Voris launched an eighty–four–foot sloop, the *Nelson,* for a party in Croton. In the spring of 1851 Robert Felter built a sloop of like size at his Upper Nyack shipyard, while another boss carpenter, Abram Polhamus, supervised the construction of a second sloop at his Nyack ways.[6]

Dickey and Voris, together with James Edmund Smith, were the three leading ship carpenters in the Nyack area from 1850 to 1870. Dickey had been born at the Nyack landing in 1808. He was the son of George Dickey, an English ship captain and builder who had made his home in the neighborhood sometime earlier. Dickey grew up at Nyack during the period when it was largely agricultural and married a local girl, a descendant of one of the first settlers in Rockland. In addition to building ships, Dickey was also active in Democratic politics. For several years during the Civil War period, he served as Supervisor of Orangetown. As a man of local family roots and also as a successful Nyack businessman, he was respected by both the old and the new. Compromise between back–country Rockland, which was strongly opposed to the war, and the village enterprisers, who supported the maintenance of the Union, was exceedingly difficult to arrange at the time, and Dickey settled for something closer to co-existence with a concentration on local issues. At first he was severely castigated for his policies by the *Journal.* It was fiercely pro–Union, quite out of tune with the majority of Rockland's population. But later the paper complimented him in its columns for his sensible approach to the divisive conflict. In Rockland almost no one seems to have been concerned about slavery *per se.*

6. *Rockland County Journal,* October 26, 1850, March 29, and April 5, 1851.

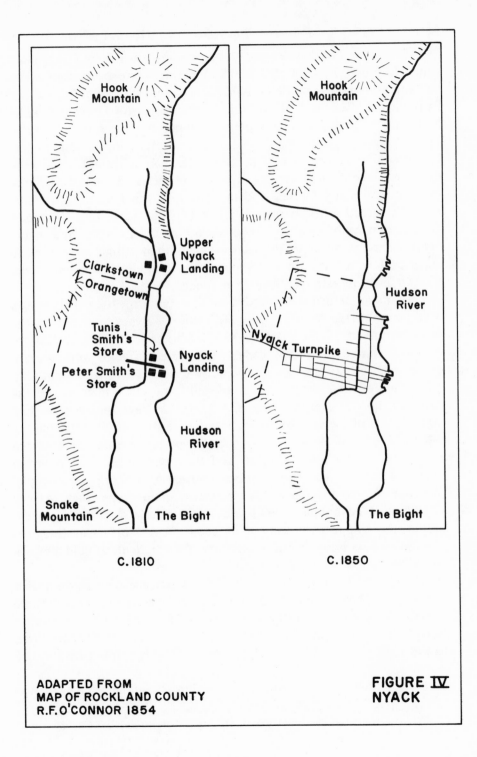

C. 1810

C. 1850

FIGURE IV
NYACK

The second of the important boatbuilders was a New Jersey man, James B. Voris. Born in 1810, he had already learned his trade when he came to Nyack to settle in 1835. Voris, too, married a Nyack girl. In the early fifties he built ships in partnership with Dickey; later he built many fine boats on his own at Upper Nyack. James Edmund Smith, the youngest of the three, was entirely a local man, having been born in Upper Nyack in 1829. He was a distant relative of Captain Isaac Smith. At the age of 13 James Edmund was apprenticed to Henry Gesner and in 1850 was still learning his trade. Later he served as foreman in William Dickey's yard. In 1867 Smith purchased ways of his own at Nyack and for twenty years built many boats, including some of the fastest yachts then sailing on American waters. Thus, all three had deep roots in Rockland, either by virtue of their own ancestry or through marriage.

In manufacturing we find a similar pattern. John Tallman, a descendant of the first European to settle at Nyack, had begun the manufacture of pianos there in 1832. Abraham and Henry Storms, who had started producing cedar pails there in 1840, were descendants of Dirck Storms, the first County Clerk of Orange County. In 1850 each of these workshops employed some seven men, as did the carriage shop of Aaron Christie. Christie, a New Jersey man, had married one of the Gesner daughters after settling at Nyack some ten years earlier. All of these small workshops fall somewhere between family enterprises and factories, and their employees were a mixed group of kinfolk, old Rocklanders, and ex–New York City people, plus one or two from overseas. While small in scope, they derived considerable advantage from Nyack's commercial location. For example, the pail factory secured its cedar from North Carolina and Florida and its hoops from Waterbury, Connecticut. It sold its products throughout the United States and Europe.

The manufacture of women's and children's shoes was the major industry not directly related to commerce at Nyack. Shoemaking there was still very much a cottage industry in 1850. Many back–country farmers from the fields behind the Palisades devoted their spare time, as did their wives, and their children, to the shoemaking trade.[7] For

7. *Rockland County Journal,* August 5, 1854. From a column entitled "Rambles Around Rockland County": "One thing which has forcibly struck me in my rambles through Clarkstown is the prodigious number of shoe makers to be met in every direction. From nearly every other house, on the average, comes

special work the manufacturer, who was primarily a factor handling leather, lasts, and semi–finished goods, took his stock to one of the Nyack cordwainers for processing. When completed the shoes were carried to New York City for sale. William Perry, who came from an old Rockland family and who had introduced shoe manufacturing to the village some twenty years earlier, was a great booster and was very enthusiastic about its potential. According to Dr. Green, in his "Notes on Nyack," "He kept urging the large manufacturers in Newark and New York to move to Nyack." As inducements he offered, "the close connection between these places by steam, the low rents and leases in Nyack and the willingness of the inhabitants to lend financial assistance." Through his efforts Daniel Burr of New York, a distant relative of Aaron Burr's, moved to Nyack and began factoring shoes there. In time he and his sons operated one of the largest establishments in the hamlet.

Several of the merchants in town had begun to narrow the range of their services in 1850, and the first specialty shops had already made their appearance. A jewelry store, a bakery or two, a couple of tin stores, and three or four groceries could be found among the dozen or so stores clustered at the squares and along Burd Street, Main Street, and Broadway. But specialization in services had not as yet assumed a major role in commercial life in the village, and many instances of old ways of doing business still survived.

The three most prominent stores in Nyack were of a piece with the old and continued to handle an assortment of all the kinds of goods a farmer might require.[8] Although the storekeeper James Clark advertised drugs as his specialty, dry goods, groceries, crockery, glassware, fancy articles, perfume, flour, and ham could also be purchased at his place of business. At Demarest and De Pew's, a similarly broad assortment was featured. They specialized in lumber and as an extra inducement to customers, added a note to the effect that they would accept meal and wood in exchange for goods purchased. The third general store, D. D. & T. Smith's, was the largest merchandising

the sound of his hammer and his lap stone, and his good natured song. . . . Judging from appearance this department of trade must add considerable to the pecuniary revenue of Rockland County."

8. We can only guess at the comparative size and significance of these stores. All three engaged in heavy advertising campaigns in 1850 and 1851, and in addition, were the only ones mentioned in the *Rockland County Journal* as carrying a broad selection of goods.

enterprise in Rockland County. Its extensive establishment was most conveniently located down at the steamboat dock. The Smiths offered just about everything for sale. Their establishment also maintained good freight connections with all the Hudson River ports.

Again, with these merchants as with the other entrepreneurs of Nyack, the connection with Rockland's back–country past was strong. The Smiths, of course, were the brothers of Captain Isaac and handled the mercantile end of the family enterprises at the landing place. Daniel Demarest and Peter De Pew were both descendants of the Huguenots who had settled in Rockland and North Jersey as farmers early in the eighteenth century. Of Clark, little is known, as he left Nyack shortly after 1850 to seek his fortune elsewhere. But we do know that he was a descendant of Daniel De Clarke, who settled at Tappan along with the Blauvelts and the Smiths in 1686, and who gave his name to Clarkstown. Thus James Clark also had roots deep in the back country behind Nyack. Even though twenty–five years had passed since the Rocklanders had begun to congregate at the landing place, natives of the county still continued to play most important roles in village economic affairs.[9]

The situation in Nyack in 1850 was in constant flux, however, and the individuals mentioned are only those who were active at one moment. The identity of the enterprisers changed constantly as the history of the place unfolded. After James Clark left town his store was taken over by E. B. Johnson. The latter reorganized the place, transforming it into a combination store and shoe factory. With shoe manufacturing as its focus, the store attracted many customers who had come to trade the shoes they produced in their cottage shops for goods. Through this store–factory combination, Johnson, previously a local school teacher, in time dominated the shoe production in Nyack.

Shortly after 1850 Demarest and De Pew dissolved their partnership so that De Pew could be free to concentrate on a new venture, the introduction of viticulture to Nyack. Through his efforts some eight or ten vineyards were in operation on the hillsides above the hamlet

9. This active role by the descendants of old Rockland holds for later periods also. In 1860 the two most enterprising merchants in Nyack were William Voorhis and Edwin Palmer. Both were the sons of Clarkstown farmers. Cf. *Rockland County Journal*, January and February, 1860, especially the advertisements. Shortly after the Civil War began, Voorhis moved to New York City to seek his fortune. He found it, too, and returned to Nyack later as a very wealthy man. Later he used this wealth to sponsor new enterprises in Nyack.

by 1860. Demarest continued to operate the store and eventually specialized in lumber and hardware.

One does not find the same concentration of old names in the newer, more specialized merchandising establishments. Yet even in these stores there were strands connecting the new with the old. Frequently the active young men who came to Nyack in the 1850s for some now–forgotten reason had settled there to buy and sell and had married the daughters of their predecessors. In this manner the links between the past and the permutating present persisted.

Among the new men who were to play important roles in the subsequent business history of the place was Richard P. Eells who came to Nyack from Massachusetts in 1841. By 1850 Eells was the owner of the Union Building, at that date the largest commercial structure in the village. He ran a tinware and stove store on the first floor of the building and let out the other floors. Eells was married to an Onderdonk, the daughter of a Dutch family that had settled at Piermont in 1736.

W. B. Collins, the first jeweler at Nyack, came there from New Jersey in 1842. A penniless youth, he applied himself industriously and shortly was able to set up in business repairing watches and clocks in a shop on Main Street. He was the husband of the former Elizabeth Cornelison of South Nyack. She was a direct descendant of the original owner of the Nyack Patent. Another of the specialty shop men, David Cranston, originally of Scotland and for many years the leading dry goods merchant in the village, was married to a daughter of the Blauvelt family. And so it went. The story was re-iterated many times over. The new blood and the old blood inter-mingled, and through this intermingling the past was united to the future.

In 1850 Nyack was still a young village. A very small and intimate hamlet, it was possible for the householders and tradesmen there to know all their neighbors. The very real problems associated with urban living were not as yet apparent nor were the accommoda-tions which, eventually, they were to require. It had been a merchant village for twenty–five years at most, and its possible future as a factory town was still pending. Many individuals continued to pursue trades in their own homes, and often precise distinctions between manufacturing, handicraft, and middleman activities were not pos-sible. Specialization in merchandising had begun to develop but was little advanced. The drug store sold groceries as well as perfume. The tin store made stoves and also sold brand new articles on a distributorship basis. It also took rags and old paper in exchange for goods. And Aaron Christie's carriage shop, the local progenitor of the modern automobile dealership, was entirely self–sufficient. The carriages it sold were hand–built.

The village continued to offer attractive opportunities to the ambitious, and each week in 1850 saw new faces in the throng at the landing place—new people who seemed to be filled with much the same kinds of hope and caught up in the same spirit of enterprise that had brought people there earlier. Wealth had not as yet produced any significant cleavages, and among the business people, at least, a measure of status equality prevailed. In Nyack, as in the world of Horatio Alger, the boss's daughter was an appropriate mate for the energetic young stranger who had come to the village to seek his fortune. These accessions of fresh blood continually renewed the vigor of the place, and the challenge of the future remained.

The Nyack of 1850 was a direct product of the rural period in Rockland that had preceded it. Until 1800 opportunity in the county had been defined largely by the simple circumstances of the rural neighborhoods. Although this back–country life fostered commitment and confidence in one's ability to transform the world, it nonetheless offered little scope for grand deeds. Then, early in the nineteenth century, an opportunity of a different sort and scale invaded the rural scene and reshaped local ambition. Villages providing many unique opportunities for immediate exploitation appeared at the nexus points of trade in the county. Nyack was one such place, Piermont another.

The sons of the old back country were drawn to these villages by the glitter of opportunity. There they met and worked with and competed against strangers from the outside who had been attracted there by the same glitter. They were ready for action and, finding circumstances that were malleable, they hammered them into new shapes and forms. They soon introduced, as J. J. Haring wrote in *Floating Chips,* "new blood, new habits, manners, and tastes, new social elements and innovations of every kind." From these efforts at Nyack, continued Haring, there "began to radiate influences which were among the first to unsettle the old established order of things." Life in Rockland was never quite the same again.

8
PROGRESS

Nyack's rate of growth during the years from 1850 to 1890 was impressive. In those forty years the population of the village increased from 1,000 to 6,000. Streets were laid out from Hook Mountain in Upper Nyack to the Bight in South Nyack. Industrial production expanded on all fronts and a number of important improvements were undertaken. The village was incorporated,[1] street lights were installed and the roads were paved,[2] effective health measures were introduced, and public order was instituted.[3]

But for a pause occasioned by the Civil War, building activity was vigorous throughout the period. In 1850 there had been only one brick business building in Nyack—the Brick Store operated by James Clark. Otherwise shacks and sheds predominated as business structures. By 1888 a major transformation had been effected with the erection of some fifty blocks of all shapes and sorts. During the year 1891 alone, four brick blocks were built, and in the five years preceding, 209 buildings of all types had been constructed at Nyack.

1. Temporarily from 1872 until 1877, *Rockland County Journal,* October 19, 1872 and August 11, 1877, and permanently since 1883, *Ibid.,* March 3, 1883.
2. Sidewalks were the subject of the second meeting of the village board during its first incorporation. At the fifth meeting it was decided that the village should acquire fifty street lights. *Minutes of the Village of Nyack, First Incorporation,* March 18, 1874.
3. *Ibid.,* February 7, 1873. On that date the ordinance establishing a police force and defining its duties was published.

Opportunities for conspicuous consumption had multiplied over the forty years, and the proliferation of service units designed to satisfy fashionable needs was impressive. In place of the single weekly of 1850, four newspapers were being published at Nyack in 1890, and one of these appeared daily. The number of jewelry stores had increased from one to three; drug stores, from one to six. Several other specialties which previously had not even existed, such as photography, now supported shops of their own. Large boarding hotels catering to summer guests dotted the landscape. Four private schools shared local pupils with the public schools, as well as attracting students from outside the community. Two opera houses featured traveling companies with nationwide reputations and eleven secret societies also found local support.

While shoe manufacturing in Nyack was still a cottage industry closely connected to commercial development in 1850, by 1890 a change had taken place and a fully developed factory system had replaced the simple workshops of the earlier day. A closer study of this metamorphosis is instructive in terms of what it can tell us about the transformations in the living patterns of ordinary Nyackers over the period. According to the New York State Census of 1855, 324 men and women were making shoes in the Nyack area that year. Two shops, Johnson & Townsend's and Austin & Burr's, produced most of the Nyack shoes. Both were actually large stores, retailing produce and a general line of goods. Their shoe employees were also their store customers.

Much of the work of these firms was still being done in the cottages; they had begun to concentrate their operations on their premises, however, and both had installed sewing machines on the second floor, above the store.[4] Cutting and binding were also done at the shops. Each firm reported employing some fifty men and one hundred women. The average wage for women was reported at $3.50 per week. The firm of Austin and Burr reported employing 100 women and paying them $4,000 a year, or an average of $40 each. At $3.50 per week, they worked an average of 11.4 weeks during 1855. Some 50 men at Austin & Burr's were paid an average of $8 per week and altogether earned $8,000. They worked, thus, an average of 20

4. The census reports a total of 14 sewing machines installed in Nyack that year. *Rockland County Journal,* July 12, 1855.

weeks each. A few employees, mostly male, probably specialized on craft tasks and worked intermittently on the premises throughout the year. But for many others shoe work was a seasonal, home–based job. In 1855 Nyack produced 150,000 pairs of shoes.

As befits an industry in transition, the fifties were a time of labor strife. Strikes in 1853 and 1859 disrupted the trade and punctured the illusion of social harmony in the community. The manufacturers responded to each strike by advertising for new workers to come to Nyack to settle. In these ads they asked for journeymen, independent craftsmen who traveled from place to place offering their skills for the best wage possible. The shoe magnates were abetted in these efforts to maintain and expand the cordwaining population by the other merchants of the village, who were concerned that the shoeworkers might move elsewhere seeking work and that a serious shrinkage in business would follow.

A major issue in the strikes of the 1850s was the ticket–and–order system, according to which the shoemaker, on bringing his or her work to the factor each week, received in compensation an order redeemable for merchandise at the factor's store. This order was presumably equivalent to the value of the goods produced. Smaller firms, which did not operate general stores, used the shin–plaster system, in which they offered their workers a ticket carrying a face value notation, such as "good for 5 cents," in lieu of cash. Such tickets presumably permitted the holder to trade at any store in Nyack and kept business at home. Potentially, both these systems of compensation were subject to much abuse by the manufacturers. For example, when the store–keeping factor was short of goods he would offer to repurchase the orders at a discount. The worker stood the loss. Shin plasters, for their part, were often of dubious value, for their intrinsic value was founded on the credit rating of the issuing manufacturer. These small firms tended towards ephemeral existences and frequently were short of funds with which to back the tickets they issued.

In reflecting on the strikes of the 1850s the newspaper, in its editorials, generally called for good faith and a reasonable attitude on the part of the contending parties and almost always concluded with the prediction that, in time, these would prevail. During the strike of 1853 the workers, for their part, responded to the public clamor for moderation with a resolution giving voice to their complaints and the *Journal,* consistent in its policy of seeking common ground, published the text.

The resolution began with a claim that in former years the shoe worker's product had commanded "a respectable position among the arts, trades, and manufactures." Continuing with the assertion that in recent years (1850–53) high shoe prices had attracted "a class of speculative adventurers" into the trade and hence, it stated that now a ruinous competition existed. As "those vampires" had allowed the love of gain to absorb all the higher considerations which spring "from the relation existing between the employed and the employer," the price of labor at Nyack had been forced down to a level where the laborer was no longer able to secure the blessings of life. A bond of social responsibility, which ought to have existed between employer and employed, had been severed and the workers victimized. In the resolutions themselves the strikers maintained that all men were created free and equal and then declared that society had no right to place any man in a condition where he was at the mercy or disposal of another. A paramount right to just compensation for the full value of labor performed was championed, and those who sought to secure a larger share of the market through the sale of goods at a sacrifice were condemned as enemies of the trade.

The publication of this potpourri, drawing values from the guild tradition, with its stress on dependency relations, as well as from the freedom–emphasizing frontier, was the beginning and the end of the collective effort of the Nyack cordwainers to explain their predicament. In all later strikes the mass was mute, and with the exception of a single individual, a cottage worker from Clarkstown named Martin Knapp, no one gave voice to the protests of labor. Instead, the strike, when it occurred, was expected to speak for itself.

According to the 1860 census, shoe work was the largest single category of male employment at Nyack. Whereas in 1850 only 28 individuals had described themselves as shoemakers or cordwainers, a decade later in 1860 the combined category of makers, dealers, binders, and cutters included 132 men. In addition, three women listed themselves as shoebinders.[5] More than 40 percent of the shoe workers reported a birthplace other than New York and New Jersey.

5. Altogether, 103 women listed occupations in 1860, mostly as servants (78) or as seamstresses and milliners. Fifty-seven of those listed as servants were foreign born.

In contrast, only two of the 47 individuals engaged in the boat–related trades had been born beyond the boundaries of the two states. For a comparison reflecting these and other developments see Table IV, on page 103, in conjunction with Table I, page 88. While the relative standing of agriculture, the boat trades, and construction declined between 1850 and 1860, and that of the various retail, craft, and professional occupations which are combined under the heading "Entrepôt Functions" remained constant over the decade, employment in shoe manufacturing increased markedly. By all indications the future of Nyack belonged with shoes.

Table IV: Birthplace/Occupation Profile, Nyack — 1860

Birthplace Occupation	New York & New Jersey		Other US States		Foreign		Total	
	N	%	N	%	N	%	N	%
Agriculture	17	3.2	0	0.0	7	1.3	24	4.5
Ship Carpenters & Boatmen	45	8.4	0	0.0	2	0.4	47	8.8
Laborers & Service	32	6.0	3	0.6	28	5.2	63	11.8
Construction Trades	57	10.6	3	0.6	4	0.7	64	11.9
Shoe Manufacturing	79	14.7	22	4.1	31	5.8	132	24.6
Entrepôt Functions	168	31.3	8	1.5	30	5.6	206	38.4
Total	398	74.2	36	6.8	102	19.0	536	100.0

Source: Manuscripts of Census, 1860

But with the advent of the Civil War hard times came upon the shoe industry in Nyack. One of the leading storekeepers failed, nearly all branches of industry were stopped temporarily, and there was no place for the cottage workers to sell shoes. Many people were left in the depths of winter with no means to carry on and by March in 1861 the situation was quite desperate. At this juncture the afore-mentioned Martin Knapp spoke up—or rather, wrote voluminously —in the letter columns of the *Journal* on the plight of labor in the industrial north and on the rapacity of the manufacturers. Maintaining that the Negro slaves of the south were no worse off than the northern worker, and less likely to suffer, he declared that the white workingman was nominally free but that poverty and ignorance held him in chains. Furthermore, Knapp declared, "A class of men having capital at their command, and excited by cupidity have embarked in the manufacture of shoes . . . and by their method of doing business, have enslaved every journeyman shoemaker who is dependent on them for labor to procure subsistence." Then, pointing his argument at the Nyack shoe factors, he buttressed it with long, touching tales of the plight of the beleaguered shoe worker and his family.

Former school teacher and current manufacturer E. B. Johnson wrote in reply to Knapp. In defending the owners Johnson claimed that as long as they had had their own way in setting wage rates working conditions had been good in Nyack. There were two reasons for low wages according to Johnson. One, he asserted, was the strikes encouraged by Knapp and his friends. As long as labor insisted on its right to be unreliable, he argued, the owners could not afford to pay at a rate higher than that prevailing. For his second reason Johnson singled out what he asserted was a congenital weakness—demon rum, the taste the workers had for drink and dissipation. Thus, where Knapp impugned the manufacturers and their avarice, Johnson found the fault to lie in human selfishness and frailty.

As the war wore on, the controversy subsided. Then, in its aftermath, Knapp returned again to the fray. This time he wrote with somewhat more calculation and with less obloquy. In 1869 and 1870 the *Journal* published several articles of his in support of an effort, then current, to organize a chapter of the Knights of Saint Crispin among the Nyack cordwainers. Accepting Johnson's old claim that the broken, rum–besotted man was a critical problem, Knapp began by arguing that such personal disasters were the consequence of circumstances outside the control of the afflicted individual. Then, slowly turning the argument (for Knapp was a man of many words) he shifted the discussion from a focus on environment, generally, to the unfortunate one's way of life as a shoemaker. In conclusion, he painted a picture of the happy, rum–free life to follow when the Crispins achieved their sterling objectives. To bring that day closer, legitimate manufacturers—those who did not work only for their own selfish interests—were urged to cooperate by becoming members of the organization. Jobbers, middlemen, speculators, brokers, "and other gamblers" were singled out, on the other hand, as the enemy to be destroyed.

To Knapp, the possibility of a harmony of interests between an enlightened management and a free labor still existed and the grand object of the organization was to achieve that harmony. To accomplish this desired end, it was essential that the boot and shoemakers participate in the control of the business and share in the profits. With these sentiments Martin Knapp ended his essays in the field of social economics.

Despite the Crispins, the day of the free craftsman, of equality and a harmony of interests in the shoe trade, was drawing to its end as technology intervened and imposed new imperatives. Early in the 1870s James Ketchell built a plant at Nyack to be used exclusively for the manufacture of shoes and in it installed a steam engine to provide power for machinery. With this act the factory system, which had been developing for some twenty years, achieved its ultimate form in Nyack. Large numbers of persons who lived nearby now came daily to the building to work with a modest skill in conjunction with the machinery. Their working days were controlled by the objective productive processes. The works foreman had become an important man, both to them and to the local community. The manufacturers were no longer somewhat more skillful cordwainers nor were they primarily storekeepers who factored in shoes as an additional line of business. They were specialists who had acquired capital, or credit at least, and had developed skill in controlling groups of individuals working in unison. Confident of their authority, they did not submit meekly to challenge. When outside competition threatened profits they arranged among themselves for a wage reduction. And in response to Crispin agitation they advertised:

> Apprentices wanted. Undersigned shoe manufacturers having been humbugged long enough by members of the Crispin Society, hereby give notice that they are ready to take hands and learn them the business. No Crispin member or friend need apply. Our shops from this date will be known as NON–SOCIETY SHOPS.
>
> —Ketchell and Purdy, E. Burr[6]

A year later in 1871, the Crispins reacted to Edward Burr's plan to introduce power–driven machinery at his shop by striking. They demanded a wage adjustment in compensation for the mechanization. The *Journal,* in its columns, remonstrated against the Crispins,

6. *Rockland County Journal,* July 9, 1870.

charging that they were "haunting the dock and the railroad station" threatening prospective workers, in order to keep them out of Nyack. The article then concluded by declaring that the Crispins were breaking the law and were close to violence.[7] No further story referring to the strike appeared in later issues, and it was never clear what settlement had been agreed to, if any. In any case, Burr continued in business, while mention of the Crispins disappeared from the columns of the newspaper.

By 1874 peace and quiet again reigned, business was good in the shoe trade, and the manufacturers and their workers were, by all indications, getting along well together. Towards the end of summer, Mr. Ketchell invited all his employees to a housewarming at his new home. The Nyack Cornet Band performed for the occasion and following a midnight supper there was dancing until morning.

Martin Knapp's Crispin essays were the last serious attempt on the local front to relate the conditions of life in the factories at Nyack to labor unrest. The noble philosophy had become humbug. From time to time, in subsequent years, strikes continued to torment the shoe industry. Yet, details as to the attitudes and issues in those clashes were rarely published in the newspapers. A primary concern seems to have been the fear that labor agitation might cause the factory owners to close shop and leave town. This concern grew more intense over the years as local businessmen came to depend more and more on a village market for their trade, because the shoe workers were the largest group of buyers in that market.

In 1886 a single manufacturer employed 302 hands in his factory and produced 223,203 pairs of shoes in ten months of the year. Commenting on his operations, the newspaper, *City and Country,* averred:

> One manufacturing establishment like Andrew H. Jackman's employing 300 hands the year through is 10 times more beneficial to Nyack than a string of summer hotels stretching from Tappan up to the Hook [Upper Nyack] would be.[8]

It was also said that the best of feelings reigned at the Jackman factory as Mr. Jackman called his employees together every six months and

---

7. *Ibid.,* April 29, 1871. For a contrast from earlier years, the *Journal,* in 1853, said of the strike that year, "If right, their demand [the cordwainers'] will no doubt be acceded to. . . . If the shoe makers demand nothing more than what is just and right, they should have it." *Ibid.,* February 19, 1853.
8. *City and Country,* November 20, 1886.

settled a schedule of time and wages with them. Any complaints were held over until the next semiannual meeting. What rules there were, according to *City and Country* in February, 1888, were clear and easy to live up to.

By the 1880s there were—depending on business conditions—between five and eight shoe factories at any given time in Nyack, and shoes were considered to be the chief industry of the village. By comparison, commerce with the back country had become far less important, and prosperity in the shoe trade was now essential to the success of the village merchants. In December, 1887, a New York factory inspection team reported that 700 workers, 271 of whom were female, were employed in the several Nyack factories and that the average work week was 55 to 60 hours. And in January, 1888, an executive of one of the larger factories estimated the shoe production of Nyack factories for the preceding year, a relatively poor one, at approximately 575,000 pairs. From these data, it is roughly indicated that the labor force in shoe work doubled during the thirty–year period, 1855 to 1885, while production increased by four to five times. The 1885 labor force was also a specialist group and devoted its full time to shoe production, while many of those working in 1855 were part–timers.

By 1890 the shoe factories were enormous, multifloored buildings—enormous, that is, by previous Nyack standards. They were operated by a third generation of managers, several of whom were outsiders who had been induced to come to Nyack by local business men. If the 1880 census can be used as an index the employees in these shoe shops were quite youthful. Of the 337 reporting shoe employment, 55 were less than 17 years of age and another 128 under 25. Some 40 per cent were female. Many, both male and female, came from families where more then one person was employed in the shops.

The forty years ending in 1890 had seen an industrial revolution in the shoe industry at Nyack. The cottage shops and the lofts above the stores had disappeared and the family had lost its place as the prime productive unit. Private skill had given way to the sewing machine, and strength had been superseded by steam power. Shoes of standardized sizes had displaced the imprecise products of the earlier day, and quantity, rather than quality, had emerged as the critical measure in the definition of productivity.

A work force from the back country recruited from other states, and from across the sea had been gathered in factory rooms and taught to produce according to the dictates of the clock, the machine, and the boss. A different and more impersonal line of authority had been established. Men and women were segregated into sex groups and age groups, and sociability was discouraged. In these and other ways the social aspect of shoemaking had changed radically during the forty years of progress. The craftsman cordwainer and the shoemaking farm family had been displaced by an alien group of factory functionaries.

During this same forty years new techniques and new procedures had forced similar transformations on other fronts of endeavor at Nyack. By 1860, the *Journal,* in March of that year, asserted that Nyack had become the center of trade for the county five miles around. It had been "a result as natural as the flowing of a river in its bed . . . . Our village now contains many large and beautiful stores in which every article that taste, fashion or industry may require can readily be found." The keynote of the new merchandising was specialization. Style replaced utility in the eyes of the customer, and selling skill had become a necessary attribute of the store manager. A new type of general store, one dealing primarily in the kinds of goods ladies purchased and called a department store, made its appearance following the Civil War. New buildings, often blocks containing

Table V: Birthplace/Occupation Profile, Nyack — 1870

Birthplace	New York & New Jersey		Other US States		Foreign		Total	
Occupation	N	%	N	%	N	%	N	%
Agriculture	27	3.1	1	0.1	22	2.5	50	5.7
Ship Carpenters & Boatmen	58	6.7	2	0.2	5	0.6	65	7.5
Laborers & Service	52	6.0	3	0.3	53	6.1	108	12.4
Construction Trades	123	14.1	4	0.5	12	1.4	139	16.0
Shoe Manufacturing	70	8.0	14	1.6	25	2.9	109	12.5
Entrepôt Functions	294	33.8	34	3.9	71	8.2	399	45.9
Total	624	71.7	58	6.6	188	21.6	870	100.0

Source: Manuscripts of Census, 1870

several stores, were constructed to house the tailor shops, the drug stores, the many bakeries, groceries, and meat markets, the ladies' millinery shops, and the many other specialty shops that had replaced the general stores of earlier years. While some may have claimed that apathy prevailed in Nyack, others looked forward to a grand future.

By 1870 entrepot functions had expanded considerably at Nyack while shoe manufacturing had suffered an absolute decline in the number of male workers employed. (Compare Table V above with Table IV on page 103.) Shoe factory construction and the introduction of power–driven machinery in the early seventies, however, led to a resurgence of that industry during the decade that followed. The foreign–born population continued to increase slightly, in relative terms, during the period between 1860 and 1870. Many of the new arrivals from overseas worked as laborers or servants or established themselves in retail as storekeepers or taverners. The number of women reporting occupations in the census had more than doubled. Overall, the number listed in the census as working had increased from 104 in 1860 to 259 in 1870. Women worked mainly as dressmakers, milliners, and teachers as well as in the shoe trade where 36, an increase of 33 over 1860, reported employment in 1870.

The decade following (1870–1880) saw the completion of a railroad connecting Nyack with New York City and, in consequence, grand ambitions were further stimulated. Writing to the *Journal's* editor in 1868, in anticipation, the landholder William Voorhis commented, "If we can accomplish the above object (the construction of the railroad), Nyack, within five years, will have a population of eight or ten thousand inhabitants, and her property increased two millions of dollars." At the railroad's opening in June, 1870, the *Journal* reprinted the comments of a Jersey paper which declared that with this impetus:

> A new, energetic, enterprising, prompt, and businesslike population will invade the place; locate there; fill the boarding houses to repletion; build tasteful residences; and soon demand good streets and roads in the place of the many that now so sadly detract from the beauties that nature has lavishly showered upon the village.

Ambition's reward was an immediate boom. Thanks to the impulse the railroad gave to trade, many new commercial blocks were constructed. Most of these were built at locations convenient to the depot and acquired as tenants the more contemporary–minded of the village merchants. The resort hotels increased, both in number and in size, and as a result of their expansion professional catering and entertainment was encouraged to develop. A fever in real estate speculation spread through the community and normally cautious individuals, caught up in its heat, offered their places for subdivision. Many of the new settlers they attracted to the village were employed in the metropolis and sought in Nyack a place to raise their families. Thus a suburbanite class composed of individuals both relatively prosperous and used to authority began to form at Nyack.

The new shoe factories, then under construction, were built close by the railroad freight station and, significantly, away from the docks at the riverside. Their completion gave a vigorous boost to the shoe trade and by 1880 the number of shoe workers had more than doubled—from 145 to 337 in 1870. Altogether, the census reported male shoe workers constituted 22.7 per cent of the 1880 labor force, up, sharply, from the 12.5 per cent of 1870. The expansion excitement was especially intense to the south of the hamlet, where progress had previously been dormant. Thus, in commerce, in suburban development, and in shoe manufacturing, the railroad effectively turned the village around, away from its ancient ally, the river, and towards industry.

By 1890 the impetus imparted by the railroad had just about played out. South Nyack had already become filled with people. Population was still increasing, however, as new areas to the west and north were opening up. Shoe manufacturing and boatbuilding were still major industries, as they had been for some years, but there were also new hopes. Flower greenhouses serving the New York City market had made their appearance and in the eyes of some, reported the *Journal*, Nyack had become a "city of glass." In an effort to stimulate further new development, William Voorhis had experimented with a steam catamaran designed for passenger service, and others were talking about constructing superfast power boats for the river trade. Gas and electricity had come to Nyack as local ventures too. By all accounts, the boom of 40 years' duration was continuing. Things still looked good in 1890. That progress had already run its course was not readily apparent.

With the construction of the railroad the river trade began to decline, and Nyack's location as a landing place was no longer as significant strategically for development. Nevertheless, a commitment to innovation continued as a dominant motive in the community, and some still liked to think of the village as a frontier for economic development. In that sense everything was in excellent shape and prospects were generally good.

It would be just as reasonable, however, to take the same forty years and paint them as years of disenchantment. They had involved a drastic restatement of the terms of living, and for many the constant element in that restatement was the inevitability of failure. Concentration on the data alone conceals the extent of the ravages accompanying the concrete details of existence at Nyack during those forty years, and in so doing, obscures many of the melancholy implications of that existence.

In an earlier chapter we described a pleasant scene of 1850, full of harmony and industry, and rewarding those who applied themselves conscientiously. In it we saw the busy shopkeepers tending their stores, arranging for bargains; we watched the shipwrights as they launched their fast, handsome yachts; and we listened to the shoemakers singing as they hammered at their lasts. A pleasant image, it was true and at the same time deceiving.

The times in which these people lived and worked were mutable and events moved rapidly. Due to the pace a reasonable level of achievement was never out of reach for the ambitious and industrious young man, but to retain success was a different matter. Each new generation had its pioneering prerogative and, as decade succeeded decade, each insisted on its right to seek the top. Frequently, such conquest as there was had to be at the expense of someone who had held the center of the stage during an earlier act in the drama of progress. A conflict across generations was thus inevitable. Where the young man sought achievement, the older man was concerned about the protection of his prerogatives and possessions. These were the mark of his accomplishment, the assurance of his well–being, and, in frontier terms, the foundation of his cherished independence.

As long as progress proceeded at a rapid pace there was room for newcomers, and the pressures of competition were not unreasonable. The young had their openings to exploit and the old the freedom to enjoy earlier successes. On the other hand, when the focus of opportunity shifted inconveniently or when progress paused, the battle for position waxed hot. The possessed saw their chances threatened, the possessors, their freedom undermined. Those who could not move with the times were ruthlessly crushed, and life at the landing place became exceedingly difficult.

In 1877 the situation went out of focus altogether and a general collapse ensued. Both banks at Nyack failed, many businessmen closed their doors, and the Smith enterprises, which for so long had provided lifeblood to the community, declared bankruptcy. The decline in revenues and the closing of the shops was readily transformed into a social catastrophe. Friendship and trust were replaced by acrimony and animosity, and much that was germane to life and living was destroyed.

The failure of the Smiths, in 1878, was especially telling. They had been losing ground for a number of years. Throughout the mid–century decades the county's farm produce business was under pressure as railroads reached out over the nation and connected New York City to localities with soil that was more fertile than Rockland's. Consequently, Nyack's role as an entrepôt declined. Then, with the extension of the railroad spur to Nyack in 1870, many of the riverside investments of the Smiths became entirely superfluous. Opportunity shifted from the docks downtown to the depot. It also changed its shape. Now, the advantage lay with those offering services and facilities for the shoe workers and the suburbanites from New York. For that market, the demand was centered in specialty shops offering fashionable goods, ready made and conveniently packaged.

Resolute, the Smiths resisted, and attempted to stand progress off. They fought the construction of the railroad to Nyack. They offered inducements to the shoe manufacturers to establish their shops near the steamboat dock. They increased their advertising. At the same time they held to the old merchandising ways that had proved profitable in the past. Some customers were loyal and continued to trade at the dock, but the cause was already lost. The gap between income and outlay continued to widen and eventually the Smiths were forced to rely on credit extended by the friendly local bankers. In the aftermath of the nationwide depression of 1873, business was slow everywhere and it was difficult to keep sick enterprises alive. Trade at the store continued to be unresponsive and the customers were fewer and fewer.

Then in 1877 the Nyack Savings Bank suspended. The Smiths were caught in the credit squeeze that resulted and closed their doors. The collapse of the Smiths led to the subsequent failure of the Rockland County National Bank and the bankruptcy of many men who had been prominent in Nyack for the previous thirty years. The many real estate speculations that had accompanied the construction of the railroad faced foreclosure and the landed rich were suddenly poor. The shoe factories, which had begun operations with such grand hopes a number of years earlier, closed their doors. Both managers and workers faced unemployment. The bubble of hope had burst and for the time being the village was dead.

Among those who failed were the Storms brothers, who had operated the cedar pail factory at Nyack since 1840, the tin merchant, J. N. Perry, and Isaac Dutcher, who had been born at Nyack in 1812 and who had engaged in many ventures there during his working years. Following the failure of the savings bank, two men who had played important roles in progress earlier—the real estate investor, R. P. Eells, and the former postmaster, Isaac W. Canfield—were found to have been criminally negligent and subsequently served jail terms. Others who had been highly respected for many years were also threatened with prosecution, but no additional legal proceedings were instituted. The vile suspicion clung for some time, however, like smog on a summer evening.[9]

For many of Nyack, 1878 represented the end of their aspirations. Some few, like the Smiths, continued to struggle against what must have seemed a malevolent fate. Defeat nagged them. Later in the same year, shortly after she had been chartered by David Smith, the steamboat *Magenta* exploded and six of her passengers were killed. His brother Tunis continued in commerce and opened a grocery store at the dock in 1880. Five years later he accepted the inevitable and moved the store to Main Street, away from the landing place. Others left town in search of new frontiers. Peter Voorhis, William's brother, for one, went west at the age of 59 in search of new riches along with the young men of the time. A year after he left Nyack he died in a Colorado mining camp, a victim of exposure. Finally, there were those who stayed on and continued to exist, their later years marked more by resistance to further advance than by stirring accomplishments. David J. Blauvelt was one of these. In the 1870s he had been President of the National Bank and was noted for his efforts in behalf of village improvements. But in the 1890s his major contribution to

9. Cf. *Rockland County Journal* for 1877 and 1878, especially May 17, 1879, for the legal decision referring to the Rockland Savings Bank.

public life at Nyack was his stubborn opposition to the construction of a sewer system for the village.

The years 1877–78 were dark days indeed in the history of Nyack. The old Rockland families were never as prominent again, nor was the control of enterprise so firmly held in the hands of those whose roots were to be found in Rockland's past. The new leadership that emerged was largely composed of outsiders and recent immigrants. Notable among the outsiders were the two third–generation shoe manufacturers, Andrew H. Jackman and George Morrow. They had been attracted to Nyack by the availability of machinery and skilled workers there. For foremen, they hired the men who had built the shoe factories in the seventies and in this way did maintain some measure of continuity. Among the other outsiders who played prominent roles in the eighties, after the debacle, were a number of suburbanites, who had settled in South Nyack and Nyack after the completion of the railroad but continued to work in New York City.[10] It was primarily through their efforts that a new bank was organized at Nyack in 1878.

The immigrant tradesmen were another group whose accomplishments were important during that period. Many had made their homes in Nyack in the fifties and sixties and had opened little shops of one sort or another. In the course of time they had benefited from population growth and the concomitant increase in the demand for their goods. They prospered and invested the profits of the prosperity in new facilities. Quite possibly half of all the business blocks standing at Nyack in 1950 were built in the 1880s and 1890s by men of this group.

The new moment of development was short–lived, however. During the depression of 1893 the shoe factories failed and, despite several efforts to reopen them later, the shoe trade declined at Nyack after that date and eventually disappeared. Other places became more fashionable and the hotels closed. While the village continued to serve as a market place for a section of the county, other villages with superior railroad connections grew in competition with it, and Nyack stores often found the going slow. Boatbuilding and servicing

---

10. Throughout the eighties the numbers and influence of the suburban commuters increased. Most of these newcomers located in South Nyack, and many who were influential in the city carried their exterior prestige into the village councils and controversies.

continued, but mainly for pleasure craft. The river barges and the coasting schooners stopped coming to the landing place, and eventually the day boat to the city was discontinued. An effort to resuscitate commerce through the introduction of street railways failed before a rail had been laid. By the time the new century arrived, progress lay becalmed at Nyack. The dreams had ended, the opportunities that had tumbled out one after another in rapid succession during the century preceding had evaporated, and the place had stopped short as a frontier of business.

And so it had come and gone, the moment when men thought they could make the world as they saw fit.

9

THE FRUITS OF PROGRESS

Winter had begun to set in. Rather abruptly, in 1893, progress slowed down to a walk, and the period of development ended. The troubles did not begin with that date, however. Instead, they had been accumulating, and only reached their critical mass that year.

Speaking in 1897 at the occasion celebrating the organization of a Board of Trade for the village, president–elect John W. Callahan called attention to the dull times which had fallen on Nyack and attributed them to the obstinacy of the local property holders:

> . . . Many years ago Nyack was a place much sought after by manufacturers, and several great concerns like the Singer Manufacturing Company, now located at Elizabeth, New Jersey, made serious efforts to locate themselves here. . . .
> We are forced to say impartially and truthfully that these great concerns were met with a spirit of avarice and overreaching by our owners of land so strong that it forced these would–be sojourners amongst us to give up the idea of locating here, and thus gave the town a serious setback as far back as 1870. . . .[1]

Then, referring directly to the depression of 1893 when most of the shoe companies failed, he continued:

> Many of our mechanics and artisans have been forced after long and painful waiting, to seek other fields. The merchants have suffered great

1. *Rockland County Journal,* February 5, 1897.

losses due to this migration and its causes, and have sustained still greater losses from a diminished volume of business, and these are the more grievous because they cannot be publicly discussed.

Callahan's opinions were not original with him, however, and as early as July of 1878 a somewhat similar criticism castigating the property holders had appeared in a *Journal* editorial tellingly titled "What We Need." It concluded with the admonition, "Go out and seek business men and try to draw them here. Show them you want them here." Thus the newspaper underscored the despair which seemed to have afflicted Nyack late in the century.

There is a wistful hope in these comments, a hope that someone might save enterprise in the village and a fear that that others had already been rejected. There is also an awareness that the local businessmen were no longer themselves in command of the fate of their community. Instead, it was assumed that if they were to improve circumstances, they would have to seek elsewhere and pray for help. God's grace had been withdrawn from the village people, so it seemed, and they had become dependents of the larger world. The excitement had moved on. For the young men who craved it, the best advice was to leave town and take up the quest somewhere else. The grand opportunities of the age were identified with the continent that had been won and the industrial system that had emerged as a partial consequence of this winning. In terms of the greater world Nyack had become a backwater lacking opportunities to fuel aspiration.

Nevertheless, absence of opportunity alone did not account for the gloom, and something impressive or even lovely might still have transpired had not assurance withered at the landing place. For a change in people parallel to the change in circumstances had taken place, a change marked by a transformation in the quality of experience and a decline in confidence. Distrust infected social relationships and people were given too readily to calumny and doubt.

The first years at Nyack had been sunny. During the forties, the fifties, and the sixties potentially capable men, many of whom were the descendants of the back—country farmers, found at Nyack a chance to strut and roar and make their personal mark on life. Caught up in the creative ferment of building empires on the economic frontier, they pioneered with gusto. The fruits of this eruption of vitality were the burgeoning village and the lively trade routes that penetrated deep into the back country.

During the early building years, life in the village must have been thoroughly satisfying for the highly charged men who came there to hunt their fortunes. Command in unique ventures was accessible to anyone with vigor, accomplishments warranted pride, and rewards were generous. Given the evidence from the first years, one feels that they and their families ought to have had a strong sense of achievement. In this, they were probably very similar to their predecessors on the rural frontier, to the people we sought to describe with the help of the diaries of Nicholas Gesner and Tunis Smith.

As the years wore on at Nyack, however, much that was disillusioning came to the fore. For one thing, some of the most obvious difficulties relating to the mechanics of living in an urban location certainly proved irritating.[2] Muddy streets, the result of the constant churning action of a too heavy volume of traffic, were all too common. Another fact that was difficult to ignore was the foul stench that filled the village air. By comparison with the situation in the rural neighborhoods, where the location of a backhouse or a dump was the farmer's own business, the large concentrations of people settled in helter–skelter fashion near and about the landing place posed unique problems in regard to waste disposal and public health.[3]

There were also many children, and no one quite knew what to do with them when they proved unsuitable for factory work. Without the chores that had filled their hours on the farms, they were likely to get into mischief and prove trying to their parents and neighbors. Then there was the multitude of strangers who had been attracted to the entrepôt. Frequently, they were deficient in good manners; sometimes they were downright dangerous.

Even the growing business community had its difficulties with the mechanics of urban living. In the days of the old time neighborhood store, business hours had been largely a matter of need and mood. The customer was something of a guest—possibly a farmer the storekeeper had known since boyhood, and with whom he had many reciprocating relationships. Or, possibly, the customer was a distant relative from a nearby neighborhood, who had dropped by

2. Paxson stresses qualitative differences in post-frontier experiences as compared to frontier experience. Cf. Paxson, *When the West is Gone,* pp. 69-72.
3. Some 40 people died during an epidemic of Asiatic Cholera in Piermont in August, 1854. While Nyack seems to have escaped such disasters the residents there were undoubtedly aware of the possibilities for epidemic in the crowded urban environment.

to pass the time, exchange a bit of gossip, and pick up a needed bag of nails.

In the villages, on the other hand, the merchants dealt primarily with relative strangers and in special categories of goods. Everything moved at a more rapid pace, amenities were dispensed with, and success often depended on one's ability to persuade a purchaser to buy, regardless of his needs. In Nyack intense competition among the storekeepers drove them to working long hours. A constant concern charged with apprehension as to whether the year's special line would sell dominated the merchant's daily hours, and in time, as the texture of competition gained definition, he became an appurtenance of the enterprise he had once dominated.

Throughout the period of economic growth in Nyack the merchants sought through mutual agreements to introduce reasonableness into their arrangements. In 1886, for example, a Merchant's Protective Association was established with the purpose of shortening the hours of work, preventing the adulteration of goods, and averting the depredations of dishonest persons on the business community. But it proved difficult to achieve agreement and most such efforts to secure peace and leisure time through cooperation came to little. The more aggressive of the merchants eschewed restraint, and the unreasonably long hours and insecurity continued.

Questions about decor and other arrangements in the shopping area offer us particularly telling examples of the problems people in commerce had. Each merchant in his private concern sought, on the one hand, to reach out and grab the customers as they passed, dragging them into his place of business. In the service of this impulse he crowded his store close against the property line on the street side. He also went to great lengths to differentiate his store from those of his neighbors and for this reason favored exotic, sometimes grotesque, facades. His community concern, on the other hand, lay in bringing as many customers to the entrepôt as possible and in making their stay there pleasant. In the service of this impulse he wanted streets that were inviting and convenient and stores that were, as a totality, attractive. These two sets of ends—the private and the community—contravened each other and led to conflict among the merchants. During the period of progress the villagers moved several times to widen the downtown streets in order to make access easier to the stores there, but in each instance the effort came to naught. The community interest was never well supported and generally, after a period of argument, private interests won out. The long–term consequence was a variegated collection of stores and tenements, oddly shaped and sized, jerry–built, inconvenient in appointments, and crowded tight by the desirable locations. In those sections of the village where urban renewal has not made its mark, the situation continues to this day. The general effect is seen by some as quaint, by others, atrocious. Similar problems with the mechanics of the village environment presented themselves at all levels of life there.

A second factor operating to produce tensions at Nyack had to do with the people who had come there to settle and their patterns of social interaction. Early in the history of the village its population was more homogeneous than it was later. In those first years the landing place had been especially attractive to the enterprising back–country people of Rockland, and prior to the Civil War this group probably constituted a majority of the new urbanites in the village. These same individuals dominated civic activities at the landing place during the formative years and through their influence set the main themes in village development. The many opportunities available in Nyack proved attractive to others from different places also, and as the century wore on, they drew men and women to the village from New York City, from New England, from the Middle Atlantic states, and from a number of European countries, as well as from Rockland. As this second influx grew in size, the social roles they played enlarged in scope and significance and, eventually, they too became active in civic affairs. John Callahan, for one, who was quoted earlier in this chapter, was the son of an Irish immigrant.

Throughout its history there had been a steady stream of immigration into Rockland. But the flow of this stream had run light during the rural period, and the influx was never so large at any one time that it could not be assimilated into the group already resident there. Furthermore, everyone's way of life had been roughly the same during the rural period, and neighborliness had been a necessary element for prosperity. Economic and social conditions thereby operated together to encourage homogeneity in the population during the period of settlement prior to 1830.

With the construction of villages at the landing places and the development of trade and manufacturing facilities, however, the area's ability to absorb population increased immensely and the total population to be assimilated gained sharply. Immigrants from many cultures came singly and in groups and settled together in close proximity. Where the individuals of a single alien culture were sufficiently numerous to form an interaction group among themselves, they tended to develop their own sub–community within the village and to retain, at least in part, their own customs. Often these groups established their own church, and sometimes, a special political institution, and through these expressed something of their uniqueness. This cultural identification was especially significant for those of German and Irish extraction, and for the Old Dutch who had come out of the back country in Rockland.

Through the new immigration, small but systematic discontinuities developed between culture groups. Each of the peoples that settled in Nyack retained some of the alien qualities it had brought to the village. The maintenance of such cultural insularity was made possible by the village situation, where the numbers in a given group were sufficiently large to provide a range of interactions and where the members lived close enough to reinforce each other. These stood as obstacles to the assimilation of the newer urbanites into the general culture in Nyack. Thus, instead of a social order in which the artificial accumulations of the past "fell away" and left people free to develop entirely new attributes, questions of tradition and social standing remained to color their new existences. While peoples were mixed together at Nyack, the mixture remained lumpy; consequently, folkways and customs more appropriate to their places of origin survived.

Emerging industrialism also operated to create and accentuate discontinuities within the community. In the urban environment the labor force was enabled, in fact, constrained, to obtain its incomes through occupational specialization. Role differentiation replaced the continuity and integration of activity that had been characteristic of the farm homestead. The hired hand, a helpmeet who roomed in the main house or the barn and ate at the farmer's table, gave way to the specialist who worked within defined limits for a cash income. In this new work situation sociability *per se* grew vestigial. People experienced each other in segmented roles, and these roles were the signal feature of their interaction. Mobility between occupations, which had been marked in the early days in Nyack, and commonplace in the back country, declined considerably. Shoe workers confined their efforts to the business of producing shoes, and merchants became, more and more, experts in the handling of a particular line of goods.

In the ordinary course of events, the men and women who comprised a single occupational category met and worked together. In time occupational groups, bound together by face–to–face interactions and common associations and objectives, developed their own internal unity—which was to some degree separate and distinct from that of the society surrounding them.[4] To the degree that these occupational groups defined income levels, a "class situation," in the sense Max Weber used the term had some opportunity to develop. Through these processes of occupational group formalization and class stratification, distinctions among the members of the community became more sharply defined.

In many cases there was a correspondence between culture groups and class groups and, consequently, the awareness of alienism was strengthened, tendencies towards estrangement were reinforced, and the social technique of measuring and responding to status was made more efficient. Thus, as the village developed in technical elaboration, the old–time homogeneity of the population gave way, and class and status distinctions gained in significance.

As a corollary to this hardening heterogeneity, the anxieties precipitated by the urban situation came to be defined in terms of the emerging class and status categories. Alien activities, especially, came to stand for unique, and, in the minds of some, unsavory features. Eventually the social distinctions themselves came to carry an invidious load. A fund of mutual distrust and contempt accumulated, growing like a cancer on the social body as time went on. It spread from issue to issue, added fuel for anger and anguish, and magnified difficulties pertaining to disorder in the community.

Economic insecurity was a third source of distress in the urban social situation. Opportunity, that fair lady who had attracted so many enterprising individuals to Nyack, proved both fickle and an exceedingly hard and unsentimental taskmistress. In previous chapters we mentioned the business disasters of 1877–78, when many

4. Cf. news story on Nyack Merchant's Protective Association, *City and Country,* July 24, 1886, on the Knights of Labor in Nyack, *Ibid.,* April 2, 1886, on the Building Association for Nyack Mechanics, *Ibid.,* August 7, 1886, and the Carpenter's Union, *Rockland County Journal,* December 24, 1887.

of the leading business enterprises of the village had had to close their doors. Failure was an all–too–common event in the shoe business and over the course of the nineteenth century almost every manufacturer operating in Nyack faced bankruptcy at least once. Other enterprises encountered a similar fate. In the back country, a man in retreat could always make a go of it on his farm (was not this the meaning of self–sufficiency), but in the village there was no final line of defense. When a family moved to the village they became dependents of an impersonal force, the market, which had no sympathetic concern for their needs and desires. Frequently, the rewards the market offered for the services of the family members were handsome. But when circumstances turned, they were often left destitute, with no resources other than the charity of their neighbors to fall back on. When the business crisis was general in the community, the situation could be especially tormenting.

As long as prosperity prevailed, the exasperating difficulties with mechanical arrangements, the growing heterogeneity of the population and the pressures of competition, however unpleasant, were at least tolerable. But progress continued, population increased, and further problems accumulated. They were a constant source of concern and a challenge to those who liked to think they were leaders in the community. In time, improvement became something of a credo with the active people of Nyack. By improvement they meant the setting right of apparent wrongs. Writing in June, 1877, the editor of the *Journal* gave voice to this credo when commenting on the virtues of inquiry:

> We seek to encourage proper inquiry. Our effort as a county lies in the neglece of it. . . . Is it not a fact, defying dispute, that the moment any community awakens to the why or wherefore of any deficiency, they soon arrive at the cause of it and apply the remedy.

The self–chosen leaders of Nyack, who were also in most cases its business leaders, set about dealing with the wrongs they identified in terms they were used to and understood. They approached the problems engendered by crowd living in a manner that was hopeful, righteous, practical, energetic, self–absorbed, and sometimes ruthless, and in their solutions they applied techniques similar to those which had worked for them in business. Most often they acted only in re sponse to an acknowledged crisis, with *ad hoc* solutions tinged with personal identification. Large but not necessarily consistent plans, combined with personal energy and insufficient means, were a constant companion of these efforts. Opposition to improvement, when it appeared, was made of much the same personality cloth from which advocacy had been cut; hence, the effort to right an apparent wrong was usually accompanied by controversy. The characteristic pattern of improvement in Nyack like that of progress itself was romantic rather than classic.

During the early, sunny years at Nyack, confidence and assurance accompanied efforts to cope with the crowd conditions and attendant miseries prevailing in the villages. The men and women who assumed leadership expected results from their efforts comparable to those apparent in economic affairs and worked assiduously to get them. Their projects were not always wise, however, and as the problems multiplied and proved intractable they grew less sanguine. They also found themselves driven, at times, to make dispositions contradicting their basic beliefs. And when in the later, winter years progress failed them they pretty much gave up in their efforts. It was then, after grace seemed to have been withdrawn from the village, that the gloom grew thick and impenetrable.

Nevertheless, these efforts at moral and public improvement left their mark on the way of life that was the sum of relationships there. As was true of the economy, the society at Nyack was never designed with care. Instead it emerged from individual acts that had been bent, twisted, turned, pointed, and inflated in response to pressures generated from practical needs. To illustrate these efforts in all their variety we have selected three controversies of special significance in the sense that, from what can be read in the newspapers, they seem to have been of critical importance to the villagers themselves. Let us consider them now.

10
THE TEMPERANCE MOVEMENT

In the chapter on Haverstraw in A. S. Tompkins' *History of Rockland County* there is a short summary of significant events in that hamlet during the 1830s and 1840s. Two cryptic comments warn us of the first stirrings of a storm to come. We find in 1845, "The place is filled with strangers. More rum is sold in Haverstraw than ever before;" and, in 1846, "Haverstraw is getting to be a wicked place as our population increases."

By 1853 the stirrings had become pretty gusty. On May 7th of that year the *Journal* reported:

> On Friday of last week, our [Haverstraw] peace loving citizens were thrown into quite a state of fermentation, by an announcement that all the operatives employed in the brick yards in Haverstraw had combined on a strike, and were making sad havoc among the personal property, and even the lives of the citizens. The Sheriff, having repaired to the seat of war found an excited and rather turbulent body of men, who, somehow or other, had got an idea into their heads, (to say nothing of what had gone down their throats) that working from sunrise to sunset was rather too much for one day, and had, accordingly struck for the ten hour system.

The following Saturday the Sheriff called out the militia which restored order. The next day a number of the laborers left for New York; the remainder resumed their places in the brickyards.

The turmoil was not confined to Haverstraw alone. According to

125

a July, 1853, article in the *Journal* a riot occurred among the railroad workers at Piermont every pay day. The Irish, it was claimed, were especially difficult to manage. One *Journal* correspondent described the squalor and degradation of the Piermonters in these terms:

> What misery! Here is a cluster of low huts, and around it are scores of children of all sizes, so dirty and filthy that their true color is scarcely discoverable. Here we see the mother clothed in rags, a picture of squalid misery in its worst form; there a group of boys playing marbles, and giving utterances to oaths that would almost appall the prince of darkness; while the mother looks on with a smile, and the father encourages them on in the road to ruin. But shortly a clinch ensues, and the crowd is engaged in a general fight.[1]

In May, 1853, it was reported that all 300 laborers employed by the Erie at Piermont had struck for higher wages. They demanded an increase of 10 cents to $1.00 a day. The company immediately discharged the whole force and sent a steamboat to New York to secure other hands.

In August it was rumored that "an Irishman" had been lynched by the ice workers at Rockland Lake. Later this story was corrected. It seemed that the man in question had been accused of having beaten his wife. For punishment he was dunked twice in the river by his indignant fellow workers.

As we noted earlier, 1853 was also the year of a strike by the Nyack shoe workers. Otherwise, the *Journal* had little in its columns about the tempest of the times and its impact there. Nyack, of course, was not as committed to industrialism as were Piermont and Haverstraw and, for that reason, may have escaped much of the trouble. Or the newspaper may not have been so candid that close to home: it was easier to point elsewhere and condemn. In any case, the editor made certain that his readers were aware that wickedness was rife in Rockland and that something ought to be done. Summing up his position in an 1854 editorial commenting on the murder of a Haverstraw police constable, he advised:

> There appears to be abroad on every side a lawless spirit, a wild reckless disregard for law and order, which is enacting the most disgraceful scene in our country, and unless it is promptly checked it must lead to anarchy and the subversion of everything like right and justice. Every week witnesses a repetition of some disgraceful fight, and every Sabbath is desecrated by drunkenness and street brawls. . . .

1. *Rockland County Journal,* July 30, 1853. Description of Sunday at Piermont.

In answer to his call, something began to be done. At that time there were two responses, one entirely political, and a second, which, while it used political means, was essentially "moral." The second is the subject of this chapter.

The first response—the political—eventuated in the Know–Nothing movement. Strangers and their transgressions were its concern. A new party, the American, was organized with the object of excluding alien elements from the right of suffrage, the rights of citizenry, and the rights of man. Because of the secret nature of the movement, it is difficult to identify active participants or favored policies from the public record. The Know–Nothing movement was narrow in intent and short–lived, but for a time it created a considerable furor in old Rockland.[2]

Temperance, the second response, was more durable. By all accounts it served its community much as marijuana prohibition does today. The movement set as its task the rooting out of evil at the source, the source being identified as that foul demon, drink. Drinking, of course, was a personal act by which a normally good person, dutiful and all that, became predisposed to wickedness. Its control, which in good frontier ideology ought to have been a private matter, became a public concern when certain individuals were unable to handle their problem with drink themselves. Aliens, as a group, were assumed to be especially vulnerable to the contaminations of alcohol and thus required special attention. In general the temperance supporters believed that if drink were curbed, the rampant vice then associated in the public's mind with drinking would diminish and quite possibly disappear. In this way peace, decency, and prosperity would return to the land.

The temperance movement led a phoenix–like existence in Rockland throughout the nineteenth century. At intervals it took the center of the stage, to fly and flourish for a while. Then, as the passion died away, it simmered down again. It assumed many forms, and from one decade to the next its expedient object and its objective technique varied. Throughout, however, its overriding purpose was to improve the moral character of the general public.

In the early 1850s the temperance people joined with others in

---

2. *Ibid.*, August 7, 1855. "We are no longer a nation of Americans, but are Irish, German, Italian, Chinese, French, or anything except American. . . . In view of these great principles the American party has sprung into existence. . . ."

the state to seek passage of a prohibition law. This law, named after the state in which it had first been promulgated, was called the Maine Law. In Rockland the combined forces of the Know–Nothings, the Whigs, and temperance advocates worked together for the passage of the law and against the entrenched Democratic party. They were temporarily successful in their crusade, and for a short period (1853-55) these forces united for morality actually held political supremacy in the county. The Maine Law crusaders were also successful on the state level and in 1855 a law substantially similar in form and content was enacted by legislature.

The life of this law was strangely short, if not sweet. As it turned out, at least as seen from Rockland, the law was not so moral an act as had been intended. The legislation, which was almost certainly unconstitutional, provided for general warrants and an excessive increase in police power. Faced with the responsibility for enforcing the law, many who had sponsored it began to doubt the virtue of this outcome of their zeal. Eventually they came to recognize the extent to which the Maine Law infringed on the rights of private citizens and with that understanding, they let it die.[3] The passing of the law into the void was so quiet that its death was never even reported in the *Journal*. Nevertheless, its demise signaled the end of the first phase of the temperance movement, and for several years afterwards the good citizens turned their attention to other problems.

In 1866 the phoenix rose again from the ashes. In a letter to the *Journal,* a correspondent claimed that America had finally become worthy of the name Model Republic, since Lincoln had completed Washington's work. But, he went on, this was not enough, ". . . America should [also] be the Evangel Republic; it should be the living preacher of the pure Gospel of the Man of Nazareth to all the earth; the proclaimer of a pure Christianity . . . WE MUST BECOME A SOBER NATION. This is our next great reform, the last enemy to be banished"—before the millennium, presumably.

The "decent" young people of Nyack soon answered this challenge with action by organizing temperance lodges and secret societies dedicated to the principle of making drinking unfashionable and in-

---

3. The Nyack Temperance Meeting decided not to push enforcement of the law until the cases then before the courts of the state could be tried. *Ibid.*, August 13, 1855.

toxication disgraceful.[4] Persuasion and social pressure rather than law and force were to be their method during this second crusade. By 1871, according to editor Charlton of the *Journal,* those "grand wings" of the temperance movement, the lodges and the secret societies, were "accomplishing more towards removing the evils of intemperance and breaking down the rum power, than could possibly be accomplished by all our State and National legislators combined." In a January editorial that year, Charlton wrote of "temperance, the handmaid of Religion." "Her work," he announced, "is a continual prayer; and the glad voices of the wives and children of the redeemed drunkard, lifted up from such horrible depths, is a grander and more thrilling rhythm, than words, apart from deeds, can ever utter."

This second crusade culminated in the first organized political effort by women in Nyack. Local option had displaced a blanket prohibition law as the popular issue among temperance people throughout the state, and in 1874 the ladies of the village moved for action in accord with this policy. A petition was circulated, asking that excise licenses be denied to Nyack purveyors of alcoholic beverages for a period of one year. The ladies soon accumulated 1,061 signatures (the population at the time was around 3,500). They then presented their petition to the Village Board of Trustees.

The reception afforded the petitioners was reported to have been "cool and contemptuous." It was said that, by comparison, "Even among the rumsellers of Nyack, there is scarcely one so lacking in gentlemanly instincts but would have given that petition, wet with tears, laden with sighs, and sanctified with prayer, at least a respectful reception and consideration."[5] The petition was declared out of order by the Board President, Dr. T. B. Smith, and the other members sat tight by his decision to ignore the document. In effect, they said, "Thank you, ladies, you have had your say. Now please go home."

For a period, charge and countercharge monopolized the letter columns of the newspaper. In time, however, passion declined and people went back to their usual habits, some drinking to excess, some hating drinkers and drink sellers to excess, and most, just

4. The organization of the Nyack Social Lodge of Good Samaritans was reported in the *Journal* on May 19, 1866; of the Nyack Division, Sons and Daughters of Temperance §203 on January 11, 1868; and of the Tappan Zee Lodge §580, Lodge of Good Templers on April 18. 1868.
5. Guest editorial by Wm. G. Haeselbarth, *Rockland County Journal,* May 2, 1874.

living. In 1875, Dr. Smith was re–elected to office. Despite the numerous signatures, despite the impassioned pleas, despite the weekly editorials and horrendous tales replete with drunken fathers, conflagrations on Christmas Eve, homeless waifs, and misery, he had gauged the political situation correctly.

The phoenix rose for a third time in the 1880s. At that time a Law and Order League was established at Nyack, its object being the election of local officials who would enforce existing legislation vigorously.[6] Their primary concern pertained to the excise laws. After a vigorous campaign in 1884 they were successful in the township election and placed a member on the Orangetown Board of Excise. Accepting the mandate of the electorate as definitive, that year the Board set the license fee as high as the state law would allow, required that applications for licenses be submitted in perfect form, and then, after deliberating, issued only four licenses for the whole township. Twenty–three hotels, saloons and stores had made application in Nyack alone, yet only two licenses were granted in the village.

The various purveyors of alcoholic beverages were furious. They made it clear in their public statements that they intended to continue to sell whiskey despite the Excise Board. The Law and Order League saw its chance in this opening and, after collecting evidence, with the assistance of detectives supplied by Anthony Comstock of New York, swore out complaints against the liquor dealers. A number of court cases followed.

Unfortunately from the point of view of the Law and Order people, that is, the cases had to be tried in local courts. The dealers against whom complaints had been sworn secured the services of wily old Cornelius P. Hoffman, the Ephraim Tutt of Rockland, and put their fate in his hands. Hoffman, who had grown up in the back country and knew his people well, subpoenaed every temperance supporter who might have qualified for jury duty (the newspaper said "nearly every prominent businessman and citizen") to report as a witness for the defense. Those who remained available for jury duty were allegedly men of disrepute, men who would never find against

6. The Constitution of the Nyack Law and Order Association stated, ". . . to promote good order and secure the enforcement of the laws, especially in regard to traffic in intoxicating liquor . . . (1) By the election of suitable men as Excise Commissioners and Overseers of the Poor, and (2) By taking measures for the execution of the laws against illegal liquor selling, the sale of liquor on the Sabbath, and disorderly houses." *Ibid.*, March 8, 1884.

a local liquor dealer. Using this and similar stratagems, Hoffman succeeded in securing freedom for all his clients, even in cases where
these clients did not bother to deny the charges. The good people ful-
minated at the futility of it all and finally, towards the end of 1884 as
a sort of tacit surrender, turned to discussing the larger aspects of the
cause.

The following year the newly–elected member of the Board of
Excise turned out to be less inclined towards protecting virtue in his
neighbors. Both sides showed some willingness to be reasonable, and
the town received a rich reward for the poor fund when the returns
from the sharply increased license fee had been paid into the treasury.
Most of the applications that year were granted.

During the forty years of progress, then, the phoenix had risen
three times. Three times righteousness, certain of its virtue, had moved
to act. Three times, it seemed, the "good" people were to prevail.
But three times they had to retreat, as the community settled back into
indifference again. What was going on?

The Maine Law controversy of the 1850s provides us with the
richest source of material for analyzing the rationale behind the
temperance movement in Rockland. The correspondents to the *Rockland County Journal* were very active during this period. The editor
at that time, W. G. Haeselbarth, was a firm advocate both of temperance and of discussion. He encouraged the exchange of opinions by
his readers.

During the political campaign of 1853 the temperance supporters set forth their position in a general statement. Their announcement began, "A moral and social evil of giant stature, and daily
augmenting strength exists in our midst." After commenting on the
decay of public and private virtue occasioned by this pollutant, the
statement continued with the claim that "It is at the bottom of fully
nine–tenths of all murders, homicides, arsons, burglaries, assaults,
riots, brawls, vices, and immoralities which crowd our jails and erect
gallows and curse the land." Several other indecencies followed together with the assertion that "it" destroys human affection. "It is the
most fruitful source of poverty, pauperism, ignorance, shame, suffering, and disgrace, known in the world." And finally, a most odious
consequence, "it occasions AT LEAST THREE–QUARTERS OF ALL YOUR
TAXES." The source of this iniquity, of which evil—physical, social,

and moral—is the sole result, this mighty curse was "the LIQUOR TRAFFIC."[7]

Intense negative feelings combined with conviction were characteristic of the temperance point of view. Judge Frazer in his charge to the grand jury that same year took a stand similar to that of the Temperance Convention. He said, ". . . it is the vending of spiritous liquors—that poison the brain . . . that set on fire the hellish propensities of men, and drive them, with maniac fury, to the commission of every crime." And the same note was struck again at the Rockland County Temperance Convention in 1874 when it was resolved that ". . . we believe the traffic in intoxicating liquors to be the most fruitful source of poverty, pauperism, crime, lunacy, disease, early and sudden death, thereby burdening the taxpayers of the county."

Temperance supporters were very fortunate. They were quite certain that they had identified the specific disease that hobbled society and made life difficult among the nominally good people. Rid the nation of the satanic contamination, and the natural decency God in His grace had given mankind would shine forth. With such assurance the temperance supporters could be practical in their approach and concentrate on actions designed to effect a cure. Normally, moral suasion was relied upon for those of the community who, unfortunately, were afflicted with a weakness for strong drink. They were encouraged to resist temptation, to abandon their wayward practices, to sign a pledge of abstinence—to signify in some way their personal resistance to the demon that possessed them. The best course of action where innocent, albeit rum-besotted individuals, were concerned was compassion and a united effort in fellowship to strengthen their capacity to resist temptation.

But with the traffickers in liquor, a different approach was necessary. Moral suasion would not work with them for two reasons. First, their avarice made them invulnerable to a moral appeal, the economic motive being much too strong. Directly after passage of the Maine Law in 1854 the Nyack newspaper reprinted an article from the *New York Herald,* the substance of which indicated that in New York City alone, a vast amount of property in bars and beverages was jeopardized by the new law, and that the affluent dealers in liquor

---

7. Statement by the Temperance Convention meeting at New City. *Rockland County Journal,* October 15, 1853. The phrases capitalized were so printed in the original.

had a direct and continuing interest in ascertaining through the courts whether or not the Maine Law was to be upheld. It was conventional wisdom among temperance advocates that such extensive investment precluded any response to an appeal for pity on those who suffered. Had the traffickers any capacity for such pity, they would never have entered the trade in the first place.

The second reason why liquor dealers were not susceptible to an appeal founded on virtue was that they were often recent immigrants. Immigrants, it seemed, were unable to comprehend the reasons for establishing law and order in the community. They were disputatious and reprobate, lacking in propriety, and they stuck together. For an example of this attitude consider another section of Judge Frazer's 1853 charge: "I do not hesitate to say to you, that this traffic is carried on to a great extent in our villages and manufacturing places, principally by emigrants, who apparently have little respect for our laws, and who are not disposed to live by honest toil, and from whose brothels issue the burgler and the midnight assassin."

Invariably, those favoring temperance conceived of themselves as a moral majority and their cause as entirely justified. Consequently, these chosen agents of virtue and truth frequently found it difficult to contain their efforts within the limits established by normal democratic procedure. After all, was it not for the good of the transgressor himself, as well as for his sad–eyed wife and ragged children, that they acted? Also, should they unintentionally do harm in seeking to eradicate demon rum, it was bound to be of small consequence when measured on the scales of time against the great suffering originating in the liquor trade itself. Encouraged thus by the manifestly reprehensible nature of their chosen opponents and the purity of their cause, the temperance supporters commonly called for vigorous action to implement their program and gave little attention to possible consequences. With the press on their side each time it seemed, to the cursory reader, as if total victory for temperance was a certainty.

Throughout each of the controversies, however, there was opposition to the temperance movement, although at times it kept remarkably quiet, so quiet, in fact, that it was easy to assume it had disappeared. For one thing, the various editors of the newspapers were generally temperance men, and for another, accusation proved easier on the whole to articulate than did defense. At first opposition to the Maine Law was open and direct. In 1852 for instance, Rockland's Democratic candidate for the State Assembly, Nicholas Blauvelt, replied to a public query that, whereas he had once supported the Maine Law, a more mature reflection had convinced him that it was "an infringement upon the social rights and privileges which we as citizens enjoy." Despite, or possibly because of this statement which was central to his platform, he was elected.

As time went on, however, open opposition to the movement disappeared or went underground, probably because it seemed fruitless. The person who remonstrated opened himself to accusations from the "better" people that he was heartless, unfeeling, and a tool of the liquor traffickers. Silence was easier. The temperance supporters had the best of it. They had virtue on their side and they had statistics and a multitude of case histories drenched in pathos to back up their arguments.

Once in a while someone dared hold out publicly against the veritable flood of "evidence" supporting temperance—someone such as a crusty correspondent in the newspaper letter columns of 1854 who signed his name simply "Farmer." While Farmer was most emphatic in asserting that he, too, didn't like taxes or foreigners, and didn't see why he had to pay the former for the rehabilitation of the latter, he also feared the loss of his valued freedom. He was afraid of the "sneaking, keyhole spies" who "poke their nose into the business of others," and that, he explained, was what he didn't like about temperance.

Less forthright men also resisted the moral adventurers but in a muffled undertone. By devious and subtle means, they showed their unwillingness to join the partnership in progress. For instance, during the 1853 election campaign, a rumor was passed around that Mr. Suffern, a temperance candidate, had died. In those days of poor communications such a rumor was difficult to verify; it could easily have had an effect on the vote if sufficiently widespread and the editor was much perturbed. Suffern won, however. In another instance of this technique, which may not have been true, it was alleged that opponents of the Maine Law had packed the village vigilante committees with members who then resisted enforcement of the law by advocating caution. It is difficult to ascertain at this date whether these plays may not simply have been imagined by the temperance supporters who by all accounts were readily given to suspicion.

A more common means of what may have been passive resistance was inaction on the part of elected officials. We will remember Dr. Smith sitting impassively, faced by the earnest petitioners, and declaring the temperance petition out of order. Despite what seemed overwhelming support for the petition, and the obloquy delivered by the newspapers, he was returned to office at the next election. The re–election of officials charged with inaction by temperance adherents was not uncommon. Perhaps the electorate, in its own quiet way, wasn't quite so interested in moral adventure as the newspapers seemed to think it ought be.

None of these forms of opposition entirely explains the periodic defeats temperance suffered. In each instance the movement began energetically, swept everything before it, seemed to have widespread public approval, achieved its immediate objectives, and then faded away ingloriously. Its victories were not minor. During the Maine Law controversy, the movement, in conjunction with its allies, overcame an entrenched political organization. In 1874 it provided women with their first opportunity to exert political pressure. Each time, nevertheless, total victory eluded temperance.

In a real sense the temperance movement created its own antipode, its own opposition. The key to this inversion lay in its excesses. At times these were so overt as to convert the movement's own leadership to opposition. For example, Supervisor Lawrence of Orangetown, who had been elected as a Maine Law supporter, resigned from office when faced with the task of enforcing the law. In his resignation he charged that the law was onerous and, further, that enforcement would add an unwarranted expense to the town budget.[8] In each instance the temperance supporters became so fascinated in their zeal for the results they contemplated that they often used means that antagonized the very public whom they tried to convince. To achieve political victory they were forced to appeal to men of intermediate conviction. When they then attempted to consolidate that

---

8. Governor Seymour in his veto to an 1853 version of the Maine Law pointed out that the law assumed guilt on the part of the suspected and laid the burden of proof on the accused. Should the accused be unwilling to swear an oath or affirmation and be questioned on it, he was to be committed to the common jail, to remain there until he consented to be sworn. Accordingly, the law, ". . . subjects them [accused persons] on mere suspicion of knowledge of a suspected crime to an inquisitorial examination." Cf. *Ibid.*, April 8, 1853, for Governor Seymour's veto message.

victory, these true believers seemed unable to compromise with associates less firm in their opinions than they themselves.

With the ends of their action so overtly pure, the prohibitionists found it difficult to contain their inner spirits. In 1868 at the opening meeting of the Nyack Division of the Sons and Daughters of Temperance, the classic statement of all zealots was enunciated: "He that is not with me is against me!" And in 1884, little or no consideration was given to the needs and feelings of the previously licensed liquor dealers of Orangetown. The temperance supporters were concerned about morality in general rather than about personal relationships, except, of course, when those relationships involved pity for the unfortunate victims of drink. At the time Lawrence McMahon of Nyack was under indictment for violation of the excise laws, and temperance adherents maintained, "We have no feeling against Mr. McMahon, but it is principle we are fighting for. If it was our own brother who was violating the law, he should be punished. It is not a question of men but one of principle."[9] It might even be said that they were so certain they were working as much for McMahon's own good as for the community's that they felt entirely justified in the means they took. In any case, the temperance supporters were given to an excess of zeal and often, through their fervor and conviction, won widespread support. But when the excitement of the moment receded and second thoughts appeared to clarify the meaning of the reforms they had proposed, many reasonable men lost interest. And, with this, support for the temperance movement faded away.

An examination of who, in general, these temperance supporters were reveals that many of them also played active roles in the economic development of the county and the several villages. At the same time they frequently were identified, as individuals, with the "out" political parties. These two characteristics were apparent from the beginning of the movement. For example, Jeremiah H. Pierson seems to have been the original temperance advocate in the county. In earlier chapters we noted the important role he played in encouraging the development of the turnpikes, the railroad, and port facilities at the landing places. In 1806 he posted a notice at his nail factory in Ramapo informing the workers there that in the future it was to be a criminal offense to bring liquor into the village (it was a company

9. *Ibid.*, August 2, 1884.

town). And in 1827 he abolished the drink wage for his workers. In politics, Pierson was a Federalist, whereas Rockland was Jeffersonian.

At Nyack, twelve village men served on the Maine Law Enforcement Committee in 1855. They too were active in development and, at the same time, members of minority parties. Five of the twelve were shoe factors—E. B. Johnson, John, Nathanial, and Daniel Burr, and Isaac Dutcher. Of these five, only Isaac Dutcher was born in Rockland. Prior to the Civil War all were either Whigs, American Party (Know–Nothing), or People's Party supporters.[10] After the war all except John V. Burr, who left Rockland in 1865, were active in the Republican Party.

Of the remaining seven, three were Nyack businessmen: the carriage maker A. L. Christie, the jeweler W. B. Collins, and the real estate investor R. P. Eells. All were very active in Nyack during the fifties, sixties, and seventies. They were also sons–in–law of the old Rockland. Christie was an active Whig and, later a founder of the Republican Party in the county. It is possible that he was one of those who found the temperance movement too zealous, because there is no evidence that he ever again identified himself with it. Collins also had a long and distinguished political career on the local scene, first as a Whig and then as a Republican, but never again as a temperance advocate. The third, R. P. Eells, was active in temperance from time to time during its later phases. In the fifties he had been a Know–Nothing; later he became a Republican.

The remaining members of the Enforcement Committee were a farmer, J. D. Waldron, who owned a vineyard and voted Republican; a printer, Robert Carpenter, who had been a Whig but changed to Democrat when he assumed editorship of the Democratic newspaper, *City and Country;* a pastor, the Rev. G. P. Martin, whose politics are unknown; and Francis Powley, who had lived in Nyack for many years but about whom little else was recorded.

Most of these men had taken up residence in Nyack within the fifteen years prior to the Maine Law controversy. They represented a generally progressive business element and might be called the live wires, the leaders, and the go–aheaders of their time in town. They were trying to make a name for themselves, to establish their busi-

10. During the war to call someone a Republican was to slander him. The People's Party was created to serve as a catchall for old Whigs, former Know–Nothings, and Union–supporting Democrats.

nesses and their reputations.[11] As businessmen and manufacturers they gave their support to the temperance cause, possibly out of a sense of dedication but also, possibly, to encourage a movement which to them seemed directed towards an improvement in public morality.

One continuing characteristic of these temperance men was that they were easy to identify. Their opponents during the Maine Law controversy, on the other hand, maintained anonymity altogether, letting the Democratic Party speak for them, largely through its indifference to the claims of the prohibitionists.

A somewhat similar configuration of social forces emerges if we compare the membership of the Law and Order League of 1884 and the applicants for liquor licenses in Nyack. Of the fifteen officers of the association, eight (possibly nine) were active Republicans, one was a Prohibition Party supporter, and four were Democrats. The party affiliation for one cannot be identified. Eight of the fifteen were born in Rockland County, and the remainder in other parts of the United States. Six were in merchandising or related occupations in Nyack, five were tradesmen or manufacturers, and three were suburbanites, working in New York City and living in Nyack. The occupation of one is not identified.

Contrast this group with the twenty–three applying for licenses as liquor dealers in 1884. Of the eleven whose place of birth can be identified, six were born in Germany, two in Ireland, and three in Nyack (one of these to German–born parents). The names of those whose birthplace is not known seem Irish and German. Only three can be identified as to their political affiliation, and all are Democrats.

It is only fair to point out in evaluating the temperance movement the magnitude of the problem faced by the community. By all indications the consumption of alcohol was both excessive and a constantly disturbing factor in the community. For example, District Judge Barculo in an 1853 excise case (printed prominently in the *Rockland County Journal*) stated in his decision, "This village [Poughkeepsie] contains nearly 200 places where intoxicating drinks are sold—making one for every 60 inhabitants, or thereabout. On

---

11. Those who were better established seem to have been less concerned about temperance. Or else, they may have felt that the movement's objectives may not have applied to them. In any case, iced champagne was served in abundance at the opening of the Rockland County National Bank in 1860. *Rockland County Journal,* October 13, 1860.

some of the obscure streets almost every house has a bar." While we have no similar statistics for Nyack for that period, we have evidence from a later date that a similar situation existed there. According to a report published by the Law and Order League in 1884, Nyack had 31 liquor shops, or one for every 155 persons. In addition, the association claimed that the saloons were open every Sunday in violation of the law.

Furthermore, the newspaper constantly hammered on the twin subjects of drink and disorder. We must remember, of course, that for many of the village and back–country dwellers, the *Journal* was their only source of information. And it maintained a policy of systematic indoctrination, connecting drink, violence, and lawlessness in one vast complex of evil. Again and again it identified the manufacturing villages, especially, as notorious centers of immoral activity and, insidiously, with the added implication that it was the recent immigrants who were most to blame. Thus drink, disorder, and foreign characteristics all became component parts of a unified object—intemperance—which acquired a distinctly negative cathexis. Certainly, given the inherent instability of the social community, the absence of vested authority, and the prevailing belief in personal responsibility, those emerging as leaders assumed that they had a duty to introduce some measure of social control. Naturally, in accepting their obligation they focused their energies on the problems that seemed most pressing to them.

Three times in the course of forty years they rose to the challenge, and three times the pulse of public indignation increased mightily in intensity and then subsided. Thus over the long term the apparent form of the temperance movement was symptomatic, an excess of energy that needed spending. It existed as an ecstatic wave, surging for a while, then ebbing quite suddenly as righteousness came into conflict with ordinary concern. At the end of each episode people simply turned to other business. Throughout, however, it seems to have been an overt expression of an emerging conviction.

One final comment: it is interesting to note that the periods of greatest temperance activity at Nyack coincide with her periods of greatest prosperity.

11

THE FREE SCHOOL CONTROVERSY

During its session in 1849 the New York State Legislature approved an act creating what was then called a "Free School" law. Provision was made to submit this legislation to the voters of the state for their consideration. This referendum was the immediate cause of the "Free School Controversy" which raged in Rockland County and indeed, all New York State throughout the period 1849 to 1851.

In the 1849 referendum the electorate voted approval of the act. Opponents of the measure were not satisfied with this result, however and by petition forced a second referendum, which was scheduled for 1850. During the time between the two referenda the *Rockland County Journal* began publication at Nyack. As the tension mounted prior to election day in 1850 many residents of Nyack and its vicinity joined the controversy over free schools, using as their medium for communication the letter columns of the newspaper.

The debate opened with a letter from a correspondent identified only by the letter "C." The gist of C's position was a charge against those whom he felt were dragging their feet:

And now, Mr. Editor, please tell me why most of our town and county officers are opposed to the Free School Law. Is it because they are afraid the young and rising generation will be wiser than themselves? Is it because a good education would prove an injury to them? Or is it because parents are afraid it would cost a little money? The roughest stone sometimes when hewn, produces the best polish; so a good education will produce a fine character, a good law giver, a pious divine, and an excellent orator. In fine, it gives all that is noble and grand. It draws out all the powers of the mind and enables its possessor to adorn and beautify the path of life in which he may be called to walk.

A self–styled "Farmer"—our friend who spoke out earlier against temperance—answered C:

I have seen the day when I was $2,500 in debt; would you not suppose I had enough to pay without giving my neighbor a chance to vote his debt on me? Is this our boasted freedom? Before we had a School Fund we could rule our schools as we thought proper.

He continued, alluding to an earlier golden age, belief in which seems to have been an article of faith in back–country Rockland:

Our districts were peaceable and all was quiet. Everyone would do his share towards building and repairing; wood was brought by those who had it, and the children were all warmed by it.

"Farmer" could well have been Nicholas Gesner. He then went on:

But now comes this Albany ruler who has been binding us with cob-webs until they have become cords not easily broken. . . . I hope not for this miscalled Free School—this monster in the shape of a lamb. If this is not Socialism in its worst shape, then I know not the meaning of the word.
Vote yourself a school, vote yourself a farm are signs of the times. I hold to the divine command, by the sweat of the brow shalt thou earn thy bread. How covetous a disposition this is giving way to.

Thus, avarice is at the bottom of the demand for schools, avarice and wickedness, too. "Farmer" continues:

In alluding to the Eastern States [a reference to New England, which had been complimented in a previous letter for its support of education], with all their schools, we have there the greatest samples of immorality and vice; the teacher becomes a murderer. It is there we read of lads scarcely in their teens, advocating the doctrines of Madame Sue, a Paul de Kock, a Debrisbane, and last of all a Horace Greeley, with all the isms of the day—Anti–Rentism, Free Schoolism, Agrarianism, Social-ism—this is the doctrine of Red Republicanism which is engendered in France, and now is raising up among us.

In the same issue another correspondent took up the defense of free schools and, arguing in terms of democratic principles, maintained that "the cause of education is the cause of Liberty. With it tyranny is impossible. Ignorance in every age has proved the strongest ally of despotism, while enlightenment has ever been the handmaiden of freedom." This correspondent, who signed his letter "Free Schools," attributed opposition to the law to "the meanest of human passions—the passion of avarice." So again we encounter avarice, and this time as an attribute of resistance to improvement.

The Free School Law received a statewide majority in the 1850 referendum. In Rockland the vote on the law was close, with 826 in favor of repeal and 948 against. The distribution of the results by township showed the two rural townships, Clarkstown and Ramapo, had voted for repeal, whereas Haverstraw and Orangetown had stood out against it.[1]

Yet it would be incorrect to insist that the electorate had simply voted along urban–rural lines or according to their party. The issue of schools was more complex than that. In fact, there is evidence of a considerable amount of ticket splitting in the election.[2]

At Nyack, for example, the alignment of forces was especially interesting in that it combined the new with the old. Democrats joined Whigs and recent arrivals broke ideological bread with old recalcitrants. The most active supporters of the Free School Law were A. L. Christie, the Whig carriage maker who was later to be a member of the Maine Law Enforcement Committee, and two Democrats, William Dickey and the storekeeper D. D. Demarest. Among the opponents of free schools were C. T. Smith (Isaac's cousin), a Democrat, and R. P. Eells of the American Party and a Maine Law supporter. All of these men were playing or had played active roles in economic development in Nyack. Christie and Eells represent the nascent business generation that had been attracted to the landing place from outside the county.

1. The Townships voted as follows:

	Clarkstown	Haverstraw	Orangetown	Ramapo
For Repeal:	251	120	169	286
Against Repeal:	173	368	286	121

Source: *Rockland County Journal*, November 16, 1850.

2. For a comparison with footnote #1, above, the four townships voted as follows for Governor in 1850:

	Clarkstown	Haverstraw	Orangetown	Ramapo
Seymour (Democrat):	410	397	347	266
Hunt (Whig):	66	297	172	150

Source: *Ibid.*

Eells differed from Christie, however, in that he had invested heavily in real estate. Dickey and Demarest were both active businessmen who had been brought up in back–country Rockland, while Smith, who had been active early in Nyack's history, was older and semi–retired, and by now was considered a gentleman farmer.

The heated controversy continued in the letter columns of the *Journal* even after the referendum had been decided. "Farmer" returned to the fray, asserting in his rich and turgid prose that his main objection to the law lay in the high taxes he would be expected to pay to educate the children of other men. "Farmer's Son" countered with a statistical argument reminiscent of those so popular with the temperance supporters. He pointed out that, for the period 1840-1848, the total number of criminal convictions in the several counties of the state had been 27,956, and that of those convicted, 1,189 had received a common school education, 414 were "tolerably" educated, and 128 were apparently well educated. Of the remaining 26,225, about one–half were reported as being able, but barely, to read and write. The rest, he claimed, could do nothing. Given the overwhelming weight of this evidence, "Farmer's Son" concluded:

> I have no doubt ignorance is the one great cause of high taxes. . . .
> Educate our youth, and I do believe our taxes will diminish yearly,
> until they become satisfactory and easy.

At the district school meetings that year discussion continued hot and heavy. Martin Knapp, the philosophical cordwainer, describes one convened for Clarkstown District §5, on January 25, 1851:

> The meeting at this time was in considerable confusion. Men were
> standing on the desks and benches of the school in fierce altercation
> with each other; others were moving about the floor with hats on, dis-
> puting the constitutionality of the new school law, while yet others as
> warmly advocated its equality and justice. The chairman, from time to
> time, called the meeting to order; a few would take their seats, but it
> was only like the sun bursting from a dark cloud, to be submerged in
> one moment in the blackness of a thunder storm. . . .

The newspaper controversy was finally brought to an end by drastic action on the part of the editor. In an editorial in February, 1851, some three months after the referendum, he notified his readers of a new policy. Owing to the length of some of the communications— at that time he had on hand one letter fourteen columns in length and two others of seven columns each—he announced that it would be necessary to impose a charge of $3.00 for every column beyond the first.[3] This finished off the controversy for the moment. Our controverters were decidedly not men of a few simple words, and by all indications the severe restrictions on their literary efforts implicit in this new policy imposed a stifling burden on their creative efforts. As a result the issue died.

As had been the case with temperance, change again moved in ecstatic moments punctuated by periods of quiescence. In this instance, however, the issues were more concrete and closer to the pocketbook. The school controversy also reflects the fundamental contradictions in the frontier ideology more closely than did temperance. In style, nevertheless, they are of a piece.

The school controversy erupted a second time in 1858. That year it was charged in Nyack that the local Board of Education had acted most highhandedly in its levies, and certain of the village's more august citizens refused to pay their school taxes. The question centered on property qualifications for voters on school issues. It was the contention of the owners of several large tracts of property that the Board of Education had packed the district school meeting with its supporters, who were largely renters, and by this means had secured authorization for the payment of excessive expenditures incurred in its operations.[4] The property holders claimed that they had been left to pay the bill and that this was unfair. The Board carried the contumacious taxpayers into court, and after a hung jury in the first trial, was judged to be within its rights in asserting its authority. It then moved against the recalcitrants and seized personal property from them in lieu of the taxes they had refused to pay. Naturally, this made the latter, among them descendants of Nyack's first settlers and entrepreneurs, very angry. There was little they could do other than remonstrate, however.

In a letter to the *Journal* that September a correspondent who chose the *nom de plume* "E Pluribus Unum," maintained that a ma-

---

3. The *Rockland County Journal*'s pages in 1850 were approximately the size of those of today's *New York Times*, but there were only four of them. The fourteen-column letter alone would have taken half the paper.
4. The Board of Education for the Nyack district in 1858 was on the whole a businessman's board. William Dickey, the shipwright, was president. Members included A. L. Christie, the carriage maker; James Coates, a groceryman and a brother-in-law of Dickey's; and two shoe factors, E. B. Johnson and John V. Burr.

jority of the village's population supported free school. He added that the property owners also favored free schools, but that an issue of simple justice was involved. It was they who paid the taxes, who put up the money the Board of Education paid out. Yet, because they were a minority group at the district meetings, they were unable to exercise any control over what were, in effect, their own expenditures. He then called for a poll tax to be levied against the laborers who resided in the cottages they rented from the actual taxpayers. This, he maintained, would rectify the situation and, at the same time, guarantee that the schools would be adequately supported. In another letter, less measured in its tone, the workers in the village shops were described as the "imported friends of the board," and accusations about "tampering with the already excellent free school in Nyack," and wanting one's family to be "educated then supported by others" were hurled by a correspondent who named himself "Bloodhound." Neither measured argument nor fulmination brought about any change in the situation, however, and by year's end the excitement had declined, the protagonists had accepted the inevitable, and the Board of Education continued its reign, secure in its authority.

Thus, the principle of free education for all had been accepted in Rockland prior to the Civil War; in later years subordinate issues supplied most of the new fuel for the periodic conflagrations. Increasing needs accompanied by increasing costs generated most of the trouble and led to the greatest amount of wrangling. Throughout the years following the war, the population in Nyack increased rapidly and again and again forced what seemed to some like an unreasonable expansion of facilities for education. When the Nyack district had built its "new" school in 1851, the number of children of school age in the district was approximately 350. By 1865 the number had more than doubled. The increase continued in the seventies and eighties and in 1892, according to the *Journal,* the number of persons of school age in the Nyack district was 2,124; the number registered as attending school was 1,060, and the average daily attendance was 785.

An 1866 letter to the *Journal* by M. R. Cook, superintendent in the Nyack district, gives some details about the difficulties encountered by the school administration as a result of the rapid increase in population. He begins by asserting that the school had registered 130 more students than could be furnished seats that year, and continues with an illustration of the need:

To mitigate pressure, a room was hired in a contiguous building to use for the primary students. This room is the best and only one available. It is 18 feet by 21 feet and 8 feet high. In this room there are seats crammed to accommodate 48 children. These seats, without desks to support books or slates, are at best but instruments of torture to those little bright and harmless infants who occupy them during a session of 3 hours with a relief of only 15 minutes.

But this is not the worst feature, for instead of 48 there are now the names of 93 pupils on the register with a regular attendance of 72. Such numbers cannot scarcely be accommodated on the floor of the room in standing position, and thus obliged us [the school administration] to exclude all who could not be accommodated in seats.

After two years of controversy the generous impulse of the community prevailed and the school facilities at Nyack were expanded. This was the first of several eruptions over school expansion and school offerings during the latter half of the nineteenth century. In each, a plethora of children would burst the school's seams, or a similar problem would develop as a consequence of the unremitting growth of the village. The fruit of each such event was a disagreement between those who stood to gain from improvements and those who were already established. In this case, unlike that of temperance, the improvers drew technical support from an emerging professional class, the employed school personnel. A period of squabbling would ensue, after which it was usually decided that those who had become prosperous would put up funds for the new facilities. Each time, despite the obstacles raised, resistance eventually gave way and the school won out, although frequently with somewhat less than had been asked. By the end of each controversy the children had all been catalogued and accommodations of a sort provided for them. Qualified teachers were employed; books, desks, and blackboards were acquired, and what was considered a superior brand of education was dealt out. Then, as the number of children increased and the problems of maintaining them developed, the crises recurred. And so the interminable, nagging struggle to provide adequate educational facilities for the young continued, sometimes quiescent, sometimes intense.

Throughout much of the late nineteenth century these controversies occupied a large share of public attention in and around Nyack. As such, they provide an excellent example of the social transformations that economic innovations were forcing on Rockland County. Utilizing the wealth of material drawn from the arguments of participants to these controversies, one can examine content and ascertain the extent to which it relates to issues of larger significance.

Central to an understanding of the dilemmas imposed by the school controversies is awareness that the arguments, pro and con, introduced elements drawn both from old traditions and new formulations, and these were often contradictory. Consequently, it is not unlikely that thoughtful people may, at different times, have found themselves on both sides of similar controversies. As a result, the dispute over free schools and education never represented a simple alignment of progressive small–towners on one side against rural property holders on the other.

To the degree that any man was a property holder of substance, whether in towns or in the country, it was likely that he would be found among those resisting the introduction of improved educational facilities. For it was the property owners who paid the bill for new facilities or, at least, that was the way they viewed the situation. Sophisticated arguments related to shifting and incidence of taxation had little meaning for them. As they saw it, they had to pay out from their own labor for benefits accruing mainly to strangers and foreigners. Or, in the words of "Farmer," "those who hire a house have not a single cent to pay."

Objections to paying taxes for public improvements were thoroughly consistent with Rockland's frontierlike tradition. Property rights were deemed to be a formidable bulwark against the invasion of the person by power. As long as the farmer remained healthy, his farm provided him with a refuge. With proper legal safeguards, such as fee simple with secure tenure, rural property enabled a household to earn a living that could not be denied except under exceptional circumstances.

To "Farmer" and his ilk, excessive taxation was a threat to the cherished independence founded on this rural economy; it was the power to destroy. Under most circumstances the ordinary back–country farmer was land rich and money poor, and as taxes increased his money needs also increased. High taxes forced the inefficient farmer, who was likely to be short of currency, to borrow to meet assessments, and thereby placed his property at the mercy of the capricious capital market and its operators. For the efficient farmer high taxes encouraged cash crop production, and thereby, a market dependency on his part. They also ate into any surplus he might accumulate. Consequently, owners, who we will remember were concentrated in the back country in our earlier comparison of Nyack with Clarkstown, whether they were capable or incompetent, rich or poor, had practical reasons for resisting encroaching taxes. Certain influential townsmen were also property rich, and had similar reasons for resistance.

Nevertheless, money matters alone did not dominate the discussion; if they had, it is difficult to see how anything but a most primitive educational system could have evolved in Rockland. The simple, practical reasons the tax–conscious people of the county advanced in opposition to educational improvement were often counterbalanced by an ideological sentiment favoring education. And this sentiment was as much a part of frontier tradition as the inviolability of property. At times, in fact, opponents to increased expenditures changed their position after further consideration of the needs of the community had pointed up the wisdom of a suggested educational improvement.

It was to this sentiment that our correspondent "C" appealed in 1850 when he asserted that: "The roughest stone sometimes when hewn, produces the best polish; so a good education will produce a fine character."

Let us think for a moment. Education in an authoritarian form of society is designed to indoctrinate the individual, to mark out a prescribed pattern of activity and then to fit the individual into this pattern. To the degree that such indoctrination can be instilled through the conventions and customs of social experience, education is entirely unnecessary. What formal education there is concentrates on inculcating a willingness to conform and loyalty on the part of the individual, and on detailing proper ends and proper means of execution. Such youth–shaping as one finds in authoritarian systems is more appropriately called training than education.

Democracy, on the other hand, is more demanding. To function effectively a democratically organized social system requires initiative, judgment, and understanding from its members. There are certain ground rules, of course, which the individual must accept. But beyond them is a more serious responsibility, for he or she must also have the capacity to work out in concert with others the concrete details of existence and to grow with the society. The prosperity and well–being of the collectivity depends on the many single creative acts of the several members. In such a context education is not a luxury but a necessity for the survival of the community. And, by education, we mean that special attention and guidance that strengthens the individual's capacity to act intelligently in terms of means and ends and consequences. The government of the people by the people rests on the capacity of the separate persons to govern themselves well and their society with wisdom. Without intelligence, enlightenment, and a certain thoughtful concern for others such a society must founder or change its form.

During the rural–frontier period of development, Rockland was nothing if not a democracy. And, as indicated before, much of this democratic–voluntaristic mode of living had been carried into the villages by the enterprising children of the farmers when they settled there. Change, disorder, difference of opinion, and confusion were common ingredients of both the back country and the emerging situation in the urban units, as were personal initiative and independence. With democracy the common framework for action, progress idolized, and a modicum of trouble afoot, the best was required of each individual if the system was to maintain its equilibrium. Or, as one correspondent to the *Journal* wrote in February, 1871:

> In a government like ours it is highly necessary and urgent that those from whom government emanates should acquire the information and intelligence which will fit them to discharge the high functions of citizenship.

The society of independent individuals required clear, firm ground rules to avoid destructive conflict among its members. Education, where it defined these rules and helped the participants to understand their purpose, mitigated the conflict and sharpened the sense of social unity among separate individuals. In addition, the society depended on the qualities it encouraged in these individuals if it was to prosper. By cultivating individual capacities, education improved the general quality of the people and thus enriched the society as a whole. Finally, the society was dependent for advance—to which, at least in part, it was committed—on the capabilities of its individual members. By helping to enlighten individuals and to increase their respect for improvements, education was a force for progress.

In all these ways education was part and parcel of the old tradition. And where it assisted people to act autonomously, it was also part and parcel of the very real progress that the old tradition of the back country inspired. In a sense, to defend free public education was to defend the voluntarism that characterized the frontier way of life. It was for this reason that the conscientious, conservative taxpayer from out of the back country was often found to be supporting the expansion of educational facilities. He had been conditioned by his experience on the homestead to be both an advocate of the school and against the taxes it incurred.

In the course of the newspaper exchange directly following the referendum in 1850, "Free Schools" extended this line of reasoning somewhat when arguing for the school law:

> A feeling of self interest will prompt every rational man to sustain the Free School Law. Ignorance is the fruitful parent of crime and if we do not build the school house, we must be prepared to erect the jail; if we do not support the school master, we must pay the jailor and constable.

Our crusty old friend, "Farmer," countered by playing on xenophobia. He wrote:

> Look at emigration, how it is flowing in upon us. . . . The friends of the Free School Law say the property of the State must educate them, for they are to rule us. Mark it, foreigners to rule us.

A few months earlier in another context he had spoken of the state as the "Albany ruler who has been binding us with cobwebs until they have become cords not easily broken." He was alluding to the extent to which the state administration, through the agency of normal–school–trained teachers, had begun to influence local school affairs in directions it chose. And that direction, in his eyes, was in response to the needs of the multitudes, not of the immediate neighborhoods.

Many of the new uneducated were aliens, unused to American ways. Others were disorderly types, indifferent to persuasion, who threatened their neighbors' safety. This being the era of Know–Nothingism, there was some disposition to combine the two in careless thinking and regard them as a single problem in delinquency. Through the actions which "Farmer" feared and "Free Schools" approved, the state was offering its solution to what seemed a pressing problem. Public education was to be parent to both the difficult and the unassimilated. With compulsory attendance, improved technique in teaching, and an expansion of facilities as tools, the general goal—a more orderly society—was to be attained.

Thus a coercive element was introduced. In this public vision education was to function not only to help the individual become strong and able, but also to pacify the weak and angry. This new formulation had emerged as a direct consequence of the special problems connected with crowd life in the new villages.

Because of isolation and social distance discipline had not been a serious problem in the back country. Unintegrated foreigners were few and far between, so their neighbors were not hard put to foster assimilation. There was little for the dishonest to steal and few for the arrogant to impose upon. Then, too, those who lived around the neighborhood were used to self–sufficiency and protecting their own homes. When corrective measures were necessary, the parent or the constable was generally adequate to deal with the situation. While the situation in the back country was electric with possibilities, its voltage remained low throughout.

But more serious social problems resulted from the crowding of the strangers at the landing places. Many unknown elements were included in these crowds. The enterprising and the lawless had settled there together with immigrants from all kinds of places. Even where reasonable, like–minded people are concerned, there are sometimes problems in getting along with each other. For all these reasons a mechanism for instilling social discipline was needed in Rockland, and this was to be the public school.

As a result the argument for schools underwent a subtle transformation with the shift from the homestead to the village cottage. Men of enterprise at the landing places required a disciplined labor force for their workshops and stores and security for their investments. As appeals for the support of the schools increased with each new occasion for the expansion of facilities, the old note of self–strength and autonomy diminished and in its place the efficacy of training was stressed. M. R. Cook, the industrious, skillful superintendent at Nyack in the sixties, was especially clear on this point in a letter he wrote to the *Journal* in 1867:

> Previously—little notice has been taken of our school registers—Yet, I am fully persuaded that if all those who may engage the services of boys and girls in this district would consult the records of our public schools and the officers and teachers of our Sabbath–Schools, to ascertain their proficiency, inclinations, dispositions, and habits—in short their whole

character—as inscribed by themselves in these two institutions whose mission it is to strengthen and cultivate the mind and heart, and make their respective records the basis on which to judge their efficiency . . . such a course would have a most beneficial effect on the conduct, ambition, and aspirations of the rising generation.

I can conceive [he continued] of no more effectual method to improve the character of a child or a man than to place him on probation . . . responsible for his actions both to God and man . . . writing at home, abroad, and at school, his own history, and that by it alone he shall be judged here and hereafter. A child has pride, reason, ambition, a heart and conscience as well as a man, and why not appeal to these motives in the child as well as in the man.

Later in the same letter Superintendent Cook went on to declare:

This, then, is incontestable; that every child in this community will be educated somewhere and somehow; and if they are not educated in the schoolhouse they will surely be in the streets. Here in this school we are to discipline the intellect, to train the feelings, to curb the passions, to cultivate the affections, to inspire true motives of thought and action, to inculcate pure principles of morality, and to instill that deep feeling of religious obligation which superadds to the precepts of philosophy the wholesome impulse of enlightened conscience.

There is much more but these excerpts will serve to illustrate our point.

All this was almost one hundred years before the organization man had even been invented. It was effective, too, because Cook achieved the expansion of facilities he was asking for. Think of poor old "Farmer," whoever he might have been. What must he have thought, contemplating this turn of events? What of his vaunted freedom, his fear of the sneaking, keyhole spies? His warnings of increasing centralization, which had seemed so strident in the 1850s, were borne out by the events of the seventies. Power had passed from the people to the school and social discipline had become one of the important goals of education.

In 1874, less than ten years after Cook's letter to the *Journal,* another superintendent, H. W. Sherwood, laid down the law to parents. Three absences from school would lead to a child's suspension unless the parent or guardian appeared before the principal to explain. After all, commented Sherwood, "How is it possible for anyone to be successful in life who has not learned to be truthful, faithful, and punctual in the performance of duty." Afterwards, in another communication, he thanked the parents for their cooperation.

So, as the century wore on, the educational system in Nyack was slowly reconstructed in line with its new disciplinary function. When John Demarest, then superintendent, was requested to resign his office in 1890, it was charged that his failure lay in his inability to maintain discipline. By that date this was recognized as an overriding obligation, and to be a poor disciplinarian was to give evidence of incompetence. Training had become an important part of education, and the prerogative of the state in instilling this authority in its youth was no longer seriously challenged.

12

THE INCORPORATION OF NYACK

Nyack was first incorporated as a village in October, 1872. Prior to that the hamlet at the landing place had had no political identity nor independent authority of its own. The power to tax, to spend for improvements, and to enforce had rested entirely with the township. It was only a heavily populated, economically active place located largely in the township of Orangetown.

At intervals during the preceding ten years, various Nyack residents had proposed incorporation as a solution for certain chronic problems. On the first such occasion, in 1861, merchants D. D. Smith and William Voorhis, shoe manufacturer John V. Burr, *Journal* editor W. G. Haeselbarth, and banker D. J. Blauvelt called a meeting at which they recommended that Nyack seek status as a village. The ostensible purpose of this first effort at incorporation was to macadamize the streets at the landing place, thus adding to its commercial attractiveness. According to William Voorhis, incorporation and macadamized roads would pay in the long run, as the tax base would increase in response to the growth of the village. Consequently, as he claimed in letters to the *Journal,* "The interest of the people and those interested in improvement coincide."

Opposed to incorporation were C. T. Smith, Peter De Pew, R. DeCantillon, and Col. Isaac Hart, all of whom were farmers according to the 1860 census. The first three were also among those opposed to the Free School law, while Hart was reputed to be reluctant to open his land to progress and to make improvements.[1] Rebuttal to the call for incorporation, however, came not from them but from D. H. Clark, a resident of the section of Nyack located in Clarkstown, who wrote the editor of the *Journal* in March, 1861, claiming that Voorhis had underestimated the cost of macadamizing the streets and had overestimated the income potential of the alleged improvement. Clark then continued, "This, Mr. Editor, is but one of the vast schemes of improvements proposed, whereby to filch the money from the pockets of the honest and industrious mechanic and laboring man, who is so unfortunate to own a house and home to cover and protect his young and rising family." Thus the love of money appears again, as the root of all evil to some and of progress to others.

At that point in the incorporation struggle the Civil War intervened. The villagers turned their attention from the pressing local needs to the problems engendered by the conflict and left the mud to deepen in the streets.

In 1866 a new move to incorporate the hamlet developed out of the insecurity arising from the many robberies afflicting the village at the time. Various residents who were also prominent in business, including Isaac, David, and Tunis Smith, D. J. Blauvelt, and R. P. Eells, sought to secure a sum sufficient to keep six policemen on duty. Little seems to have come of this attempt to incorporate, however.

Agitation for incorporation increased again between 1869 and 1871. In support of this impulse the editor of the *Journal* intermittently called for action but with little effect. In one of his moments of irritation with the opposition to improvement he suggested that "those who vote 'NO' on incorporation ought to be buried in mud up to their neck." Others joined him through the letter columns of the paper, stressing especially the gravity of the delinquency problem at Nyack. One such communication in 1871 reported that every evening at the corner of Main and Burd, fifty to a hundred young men gathered and loafed around, casting slurs on passing men and women. Storekeeper Abram Merritt was mentioned in another epistle as having taken a private hand in the matter. At the corner where his store was

1. Letter signed "William Voorhis," *Rockland County Journal,* November 6, 1869, explaining his reasons for the purchase of the Hart farm that year.

situated he erected a street light and employed a private policeman to maintain order.

Nevertheless, many of the residents at the landing place were reluctant about improvement and its advocates were dubious as to whether they could obtain the majority support necessary for incorporation. These opponents rarely articulated their reasons for balking. One 1869 letter, although possibly a hoax perpetrated by an incorporation advocate, sums up their putative position:

> We find there is a determination on the part of some busybodies, who must meddle with other people's affairs, to get Nyack incorporated. This we regard as a great impertinence. They were not born in Rockland County. Their fathers did not live here. They need not stay here if they don't like it. They are free to do anything they like, but they cannot be allowed to interfere with us. If the roads and streets suit those who have lived here all their lives no one need come here to try to change things. These kind of people need to be exposed and silenced. Some are so annoyed about incorporation and railroads we seriously think of selling out and leaving, and would do so at once, did we not hope property will rise a little higher. And then we don't know where to go. All along the river there seems to be a great many meddlesome people. . . .
> . . . We don't intend to be laughed out of our rights. We tell these agitators they had better be careful. We are down on incorporation and every other kind of improvement; so called, and especially railroads. We want not to have any more articles in your paper.

The letter, signed "Many Citizens," seems to have gauged opinion correctly; when a referendum on incorporation was called in the summer of 1871, the opponents proved to be in the majority. Two hundred and ninety–two cast their votes against incorporation, and only 75 were in favor. A year later the Nyack improvement advocates began to work again on a petition for a referendum. Then, in 1872 the residents of the Clarkstown section of Nyack moved quietly to incorporate as a separate village. A vote was taken and the new village— Upper Nyack—was approved. A month later the referendum which had been planned for the whole area generally accepted as Nyack was held for the Orangetown section alone. This time the incorporators were successful and the Village of Nyack was approved by the electorate. The vote was 292 for and 192 against.

Incorporation for the Nyacks had been achieved, but only at a heavy cost in terms of distrust and resentment. According to Green's

History of Rockland County the original intention of those who had supported incorporation was to include the entire shelf of land standing between the Hudson River and the Palisades and extending from Hook Mountain in the north to the Bight at the present south boundary of South Nyack. As such the incorporated village would have included the section of Clarkstown which had become Upper Nyack. (See Map V). Green attributes a Machiavellian policy to the incorporators:

> Their design, as expressed among themselves, was to use the taxes obtained from the outlying sections of the incorporated village, on the immediate streets of the town, and to outvote the few tax-payers at a distance by those who were benefited. . . .

The plot, if there was one, is reminiscent of the school controversy. Whether it existed or not it probably loomed large in the minds of those with extensive property holdings—one of whom was Dr. Green's father. Green continues:

> It came to pass, however, that positive proof to the intention of those who were at work in Nyack was put in the possession of a resident of the upper village, and the people of that place decided to incorporate the village of Upper Nyack. With this object in view, preparations were made as rapidly and secretly as possible, and on September 28, 1872, the village of Upper Nyack was incorporated, only twenty five days before Nyack.

Shortly afterwards the two villages commenced operations. In Nyack proper, a set of town ordinances was approved and promulgated, police officers were appointed, and an assessment list was prepared. By 1875 about fifty street lamps had been purchased and were placed about the village. The hamlet was surveyed and mapped, and sidewalks were laid along the sides of the streets. Broadway was macadamized and officially named, and several of the streets graded and covered with crushed stone. There are no reports of what, if anything,was being done in Upper Nyack.

"Meantime," Green continues, "the fate which Upper Nyack had escaped, was falling heavily on the lower portion of the village." He refers here to the section of nominal Nyack which was eventually to become South Nyack. Until 1870 that area was largely rural. With the advent of the railroad a land boom developed, which was at its height at the time of the incorporation controversy. It is likely that many of those with large holdings in land did not want to draw at-

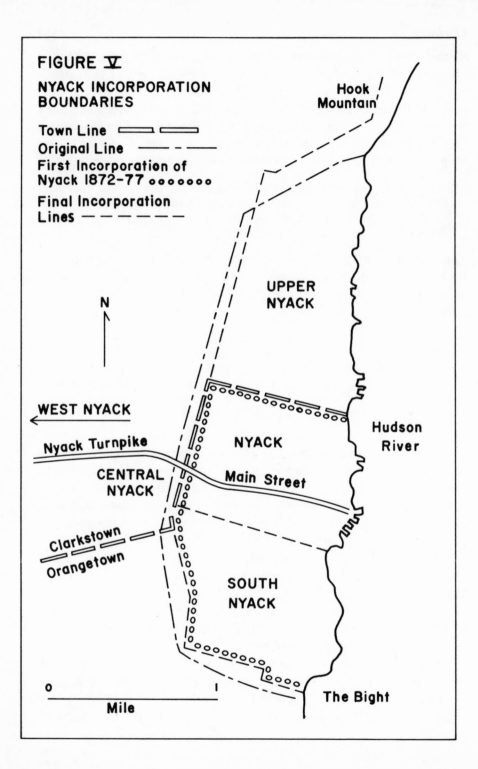

FIGURE V

NYACK INCORPORATION
BOUNDARIES

Town Line ▭ ▭
Original Line —·—·—
First Incorporation of
Nyack 1872-77 ∘∘∘∘∘∘∘
Final Incorporation
Lines —— —— ——

Hook
Mountain

N

UPPER
NYACK

WEST NYACK

Hudson
River

Nyack Turnpike

NYACK

CENTRAL
NYACK

Main Street

Clarkstown

Orangetown

SOUTH
NYACK

0   1

Mile

The Bight

tention to the taxes needed for village improvement. In any case, Green goes on:

> The heavy taxpayers claimed that they were the sufferers, while the non tax payers outvoted them, and at length [those who felt that they were being abused] presented a petition to the Trustees asking that a meeting be called to determine whether the village should continue to be incorporated or not. This petition was denied. The petitioners then appealed to the law, and obtained a mandamus from the Supreme Court to compel the Trustees to call a meeting. On the day appointed, however, an injunction was served on the Trustees to prevent the election.

· Incorporation thus was saved by legal maneuver, but at a cost. The unhappy state continued for a couple of years as the village limped on. Little was done except in a spirit of partisan combat and next to nothing that was constructive. The anti–corporationists accused the Board of Trustees of criminal extravagance and corrupt motives and constantly endeavored to force a referendum on the question of annulling the charter of the village. Prominent citizens refused to have anything to do with the corporation and in the spring of 1877, several of those elected refused to serve on the board. The oft–threatened referendum on annulment finally took place that August and the opponents of corporation were victorious. Only 71 voted for continuance while 282 came out against.[2] While it had sponsored many excellent improvements the corporation had been unable to get the citizenry to work together for the widening of the main thoroughfares. Scorned, defeated, and little lamented, it was dissolved.

As a substitute, a citizen's association was formed for Nyack. It had as its objectives:

---

2. Green, *History of Rockland*, pp. 351-353. See also, Cole, *History of Rockland*, p. 207. Cole reports that the opponents of incorporation included "a number of old and prominent citizens, and the largest tax payers, including William Voorhis, C. T. Smith, Tunis De Pew, Richard DeCantillon, and Azariah Ross."

In his younger days, when he was a Nyack merchant and not a rentier, Voorhis had been one of the strongest proponents of incorporation. However, as he was the largest stockholder in the Gas Company, and as the street light concessions had been given for kerosene lamps during the first incorporation and for electric lights during the second, he may have felt that the various Boards of Trustees had slighted him. Cf. letter signed "William Voorhis," *City and Country*, August 20, 1887.

Smith and De Pew both held extensive tracts of land on the south side of the hamlet. DeCantillon and Ross had been merchants in Nyack in the 1840s. After that decade they seem to have retired from active business and concentrated, instead, on investment.

Three of these opponents were elderly in 1877; Ross was 90, Smith 79, and DeCantillon 66 years old.

To establish measures towards insuring judicious economy in public expenditures, justice and equality in the collection of taxes, the speedy and effectual suppression of nuisances, the establishment and observance of wise sanitary and police regulations; to foster a wholesome public spirit, to beautify and improve the village, to expose and resist corruption, and generally to promote reform in county, town and municipal affairs.[3]

Good intentions were not adequate to the task, however, and there are no reports of accomplishments by this association.

Simultaneously, the residents of the southern section of the nominal Nyack, who had led the fight against the corporation, took steps to guarantee their sovereignty for the future. They hastily voted incorporation of their section as a separate village—South Nyack. Thus, by mid–year, 1878, there were two villages where none had been before—Upper Nyack and South Nyack—and none where the need was, where the problems which had suggested incorporation in the first place were most pressing, at Nyack proper. The focus of business activity for a large part of the county, it was a pocket of private enterprise enforcement, left to get along as best it could.

In 1883 the truncated remains of what had been the village of Nyack were reincorporated in its original name. This step was taken as a defense measure, to avoid annexation by the suburbanite corporations of South Nyack and Upper Nyack. Nevertheless, the new village was still not free of its history, and its leaders gracefully accepted warnings to be careful and to avoid the visionary and expensive ways of the previous organization.

Little fanfare attended the first meetings of the new village board. It was not intended that much be accomplished. At times embattled, it has on the whole continued operations in the spirit in which it was founded until the present day, as have its neighbors. Today there are five Nyacks in two different townships in Rockland. Three of these are incorporated—Nyack (the old entrepôt), South Nyack, and Upper Nyack (the two suburb villages). They are situated on the shelf of land by the river. (See Map V). Central Nyack lies on the Palisades, above and to the west of the three incorporated villages. Originally it was called West Nyack, but it lost that name to a location well to the west, across the swamp. This village, today's West Nyack, got its name when the West Shore Railroad advertised in New York City

---

3. *Rockland County Journal,* September 22, 1877.

that it had a station at Nyack and then obliged its passengers by erecting a sign saying West Nyack at the point it crossed the Nyack Turnpike. It was never an integral part of the landing place hamlet.

While the incorporation movement at Nyack may quite reasonably be described as clumsy and bumbling, it would be incorrect to say that it was altogether a failure. In fact, despite the prevailing tendency to do everything in the most difficult way possible, the immediate objectives of the movement were achieved. Streets were paved, sidewalks were constructed, street lights were erected, and water was brought into the village. What was accomplished was but grudgingly done and the proscription against vision was honored more often than it ought to have been. Somewhere, possibly during the period of acrimony, the enthusiasm that we remember from the frontier was lost. Nonetheless, a great deal got done.

More significant in social terms were certain afterthoughts resulting from incorporation. The original intention had been to make the place more attractive for business. Controlling delinquency through the police function had been a basic element in this intention. It was always clear that the caterwauling youths who hung out at the corners created a bad impression and discouraged trade. Pay day, also, was often a trial. So a police force was organized after several false starts, and eventually a reasonably efficient system of public authority was established for the village. The afterthoughts developed when it became apparent that this system applied to everyone, not just to foreigners, youths, and tramps.

The turning point in favor of universal impersonal order may well have been the "Battle of Ackerman's" in 1888. In that instance Levi Van Riper, a house mover, had attempted to move a building off the Ackerman plot on De Pew Street, although the village trustees had denied him a permit to do so. The Nyack Police were called into action, a brawl ensued, and Van Riper's workers were taken into custody. Among them were a Coates and two members of the Tallman family.

Once, prior to 1800, the Tallmans had owned a farm comprising all of what is today the incorporated village of Nyack. At that time they made the rules in the town. But by 1888 the Tallmans had become ordinary citizens like everyone else, equal with their alien neighbors before an impersonal law. As an aftermath of the "Battle of Ackerman's" one of the Tallman clan received special attention from

Police Justice Tompkins (who had been born in Middletown, New York), because during the altercation he had struck an officer of the law. The days when special consideration might have been given a Tallman were gone. Of Coates, who was also a native of the village, it was said, "No longer can the gallant veteran of nineteen battles and twice as many skirmishes claim the proud distinction of never having been arrested."[4] That law and order had not won out entirely, however, is indicated by a sullen comment printed the same day in the Democratic newspaper, City and Country: "The citizens seemed to look differently on the matter from the authorities."

In order to assure the salubrity of the citizenry special measures had also to be taken in the name of public health, and, in consequence, another afterthought developed. Again, the principle implied universal application. In this instance, which took place in 1887, the village Board of Health won a suit for the abatement of a nuisance. The victims or villains—depending on where one stands in respect to the principle—were two enterprisers from the old days at Nyack, R. P. Eells and Richard DeCantillon. Over the years Eells had generally sided with those favoring incorporation, and DeCantillon with the opposition. The beneficiaries were, presumably, the general public. When Eells and DeCantillon refused to move a backhouse which the Board of Health claimed was too close to a tenement owned by De-Cantillon and operated by Eells, the officials of the Board corrected the adjudged deficiency and then billed the two. They refused to pay and the Board sued. In all previous cases of this nature the Board had failed to prove that the nuisance in question was general. This time, however, the attorney for the Board and later police justice, Arthur Tompkins, brought twenty witnesses into court in order to prove the generality of the offense. The judgment was returned in favor of the Board. This was the first public health suit ever won at Nyack. Solicitude was again victorious, and with it something like socialism was creeping in, invited by the advocates of order and responsibility.

Originally, in 1860, the incorporation of the village had been proposed as a general answer to some of the difficulties of crowd living at Nyack. There was deep mud in the streets of the hamlet. Buildings had been placed along them with little care or consideration for the general needs of the community. At night the streets were

4. Rockland County Journal, August 14, 1888.

dark and dangerous. Rowdies milled and scuffled on the corners. Robberies were all too common, and every fire was potentially a conflagration. Urban living conditions at Nyack had precipitated a crisis situation; incorporation was offered as a corrective.

During the period of agitation preceding the demise of the first corporation in 1877, an editorial appeared in the *Rockland County Journal* defending village government in Nyack. Entitled "Organization or Chaos" it constitutes the most comprehensive statement of principle ever presented at Nyack by those favoring incorporation. Prior to this editorial it had been common practice to argue the pros and cons of incorporation in terms of specific acts and deficiencies. The case for incorporation had been composed under the stress of crisis, and little or no attention had been given to speculation on the ideological implications of the movement. But with "Organization or Chaos" we have a general statement of the position for incorporation.

The editorial commenced with a challenge. "On Tuesday next," it began:

> The electors of this village [Nyack] will be called upon to decide whether an organization for the protection of life and property, for the maintenance of order, the building and care of our streets and avenues, the security of the public health, and the preservation of all that makes life in villages, and towns desirable shall continue to exist, or whether we shall be relegated back to the original chaos where each man does what he pleases and pleases to do much that is wrong.

Continuing, the editor identified something about incorporation which he found to be ideal, something superior to the untrammeled freedom that had existed before. What is it then "that makes life in villages and towns desirable?" His answer astonishes for it contrasts dramatically with what we remember from the frontier. To him, the essential "it" was something orderly and unchaotic, something which those who thoughtlessly do as they please can wrong or destroy:

> . . . We cannot admit the truth of the so called maxim, that every man is the best judge of matters affecting his private interests. We find it every day that there should be some check on the actions of men, even where apparently the matter is a purely personal one. In communities like our own the liberty of one may and often does, trench upon the rights of another. How necessary, then, it is that we have a local organization with power to act for all, to study the best interests of all, to care for and protect all.

In the eyes of the Republican editor of the *Journal,* incorporation was an attempt to introduce a necessary element of order and decency into the lives of the people, so that they could live together in a crowd at the landing place without fear and without recourse to aggression against each other. Furthermore, through incorporation certain general improvements could be made, which ostensibly redounded to the benefit of all. Public peace and paved streets were expected to bring business to town and thereby to enrich the people who lived there. In this sense, they are handmaidens of progress.

As well as being a local organization with the power to act for all in their own best interests, the corporation was also a device to control dissidence. One of its functions was the smoothing out of the snags and creases in the social fabric introduced by nonhomogeneous elements. While this may seem a relatively innocent and appropriate exercise of responsibility, it has its ulterior implications. For there was always some element of class control intended in the incorporation movement. This intention is more clearly defined in a much earlier note in the *Journal* referring to conditions in a different village.

According to the paper, everyone was much more candid about their intentions in Piermont in 1852, when a meeting was called to further the cause of incorporation there. Several men of the hamlet had suggested incorporation, in order, it was said, to keep the Irish population in subjection and to compel them to keep their houses and yards clean, "if possible." In addition, the report continues, incorporation was to be a step towards eliminating the stench with which the village of Piermont was afflicted by requiring that lime be spread around the yards of the dwellings and that trenches be dug to lead the filth and standing water away. And finally, incorporation was supposed to maintain law and order. Clearly, the target of improvement in Piermont at that time was the large group of foreign–born railroad workers.

Aliens by definition were a nonhomogeneous element and together with the native delinquents, were the object of close attention by the forces of order and decency. Unlike troubled individuals, however, the proletarian immigrants were not helpless against these pressures; since they were a relatively large proportion of the population in most cases, they could use their vote to protect themselves should incorporation operate as a mechanism for class repression.

Thus, to the extent that the movement was actively xenophobic it encouraged cohesiveness among the foreign–born and so strengthened their alien identity. A similar process operated wherever segmentation along group lines was possible, as with occupation groups. Consequently, a social metamorphosis was one result of the effort to create an organization designed to work in the best interests of all. The frontier society of individuals atrophied and in its place evolved a society of groups interlocked in complex relationships. The various groups acquired a durability unknown to the association groups of the frontier and in time, as they achieved status, claimed for themselves the absolute rights which had once belonged to the several individuals. This metamorphosis was, of course, only partial and incomplete. The general society still remained committed subjectively, at least, to the egalitarian principles on which the nation had been founded.

By 1890 many improvements had been made in the name of incorporation; nevertheless, the conflict between the "decent" and the "others" still persisted. In 1893, Richard E. King, a foreman at one of the larger shoe factories, failed in his candidacy for the Village Board of Nyack. According to the *Journal,* nominally the Republican newspaper, the "people" had defeated him. In the eyes of its competitor, *City and Country,* the Protestants had turned out *en masse,* declaring that no Catholic would ever sit on the Nyack board if they could help it. As in the past, the old also found themselves at odds with the young—the old, that is, who held property. D. J. Blauvelt, the former bank president, and one of the staunchest supporters of incorporation three decades earlier, opposed the construction of public sewers for Nyack. He complained of the cost and maintained that Nyack was already pretty well sewered by private enterprise. In answer, one *Journal* correspondent wrote that the existing system was certainly adequate, ". . . if you hold your nose." A second maintained that Blauvelt had neglected to say anything about the unsewered streets and the many cesspools.[5]

The victory for improvement remained at best incomplete and somewhat pyrrhic. The thirty years of controversy had taken their toll, and nothing relating to incorporation was ever done quite as well as it could have been done. Throughout, there had been a de-

5. *Rockland County Journal,* September 15, 1894.

ficiency of vision and excess of acrimony. What vision there was had been challenged again and again by the assessor's book and had lost its vitality, while the acrimony had coagulated into a sticky mass. Concomitantly, public spirit faded. The village had bloomed and paled in bits and pieces, those thirty years a hodgepodge of ventures and gains, of retreats and of opportunities lost.

13
THE ANTIPODES OF IMPROVEMENT

Roughly speaking, those who supported improvement at Nyack from 1850 to 1890 were identified politically with the Republican Party. For many, this identification had not been automatic. Only a handful of the men who had settled at the landing place were Whigs by birth. Most had begun life as Democrats and had arrived at their Republicanism by a tortured path which included Know–Nothingism, temperance, and the Union–supporting parties of the Civil War period. Through experience with urban life in the village they had come to see the error in the old ways of politics and had embraced Republicanism. Or, if they could not find it in themselves to take the step signifying order and progress and held to Democracy to the end, their children took it for them. Frequently there was a gap in opinion between the generations.

Supporters of improvement were likely to be successful men of affairs, vigorous, youthful, active, and certain in their opinions about what was best for the community. Early in the period they were almost always either direct descendants of the back–country farmers or in–laws of such descendants. In many instances they had secured the initial capital they used in their ventures through the sale of the family farm.

Later in the period their numbers were augmented by those of the sons of recent immigrants who stood with progress. These were young men of regular habits who had worked hard, spent wisely, and saved what they could from their earnings to accumulate a stake to use for enterprise. In addition, a few outsiders such as the owners of the larger shoe factories and several of the New York City commuters, joined the group of improvers. These were men without roots in the village who had proved capable on a larger scene. The threat that they might just pick up and leave town if circumstances failed to please them was always in the background. While their allegiance was somewhat cloudy, they generally sided with the progressive elements in the village. In relative terms, the numbers of these two augmenting elements increased as the forty–year period wore on.

Enterprisers above all, these supporters of improvement had invested their talents and savings into the various branches of business at Nyack and stood to gain as the village advanced in size and complexity. A certain righteousness also prevailed with them. They had filled a pressing need, in their own minds, at least, when they had opened their stores, organized their banks, or built their grand structures. They had affirmed their faith in the future of the village while offering needed services to their neighbors. Practical in their approaches, personally optimistic, and confident about their achievements, they remind us of frontier people.

Progress was essential to their way of life; the expansions and improvements they sponsored enlarged opportunity in the village. Contingencies multiplied with each new move and justified further expansion, validating their confidence. So, as they looked forward to the rosy future in store for the village and to their own success, they must frequently have united the two in their imaginings. This union, then, was probably the fountain from which their righteousness flowed.

Opposition to improvement was county–wide and came from two sources, the back–country farmer and the recent immigrant. To the improvers, the back–country farmers were "old fogies," backward in their outlook and indifferent to the general welfare. In a sense, the country people agreed. Land rich and secure in a way of life that had persisted for more than two centuries, they treasured their independence. They saw their stake threatened by increasing taxation and were especially reluctant to pay the price of some other person's passion for progress. Like the pioneers from whom they were descended, they respected self–sufficiency and personal autonomy. Their party affiliation was with the Democracy, the old association of free men that had dominated the nation and the country from their beginnings. Over the years it had earned trust through its steadfast defense of individual rights—to one's farm, to privacy, and to self-determination.

Given a different governmental structure in Rockland. the opposition of the back–country farmers might have been of little consequence. However, political authority was vested in the town and county governments. During the early years, they alone had the power to raise and levy taxes, ordinarily, property taxes, and to enforce legislation. For many contemplated improvements, such as the Nyack Turnpike, support from one or both governmental agencies was required before the villagers could go ahead and act. Otherwise, improvement was only possible under private sponsorship until the hamlets were incorporated as villages and thus acquired rights to a limited initiative of their own.

During the early period of village development in Rockland, back–country men were clearly in the majority, both in politics and as officeholders. Entrenched, insular, and careful about cash, they had a paramount interest in the defense of property rights and the maintenance of the status quo. To their minds public office was a responsibility to be shared among the elect, and their normal style was an orderly succession in which every reasonably capable individual had an opportunity to serve. Lawmaking and implementation, however, were to be pursued with moderation, as they often led to infringements on liberty. When challenged, the back–country men defended their political position with great tenacity and frequently with considerable skill. During the nineteenth century they were generally the winners in political engagements, because they had the votes if not the arguments. Consequently, those who favored improvement found Democratic opposition most frustrating and with invidious intention, called that party "the machine."

As the century wore on, back–country men declined in numbers relative to the village improvers, and had they not made some accommodation to this weakness they would have eventually lost power altogether.[1] At this critical juncture they found common cause with

1. In 1875 the editor of the *Journal* estimated that during the preceding five years the population at Nyack had increased considerably while that of the remainder of Orangetown had suffered a decline.

a second group of individuals standing in opposition to improvement and progressive reform, the same foreigners who were its primary human targets. They had been attracted to the village over the years by the opportunities for employment there, especially in the shoe factories. Eventually, many of those who had settled acquired citizenship and the right to vote. In time, the numbers of these new citizens inceased considerably.

While a few detached themselves from the mass and joined forces with the improvers, most retained some form of identification with their original ethnic group. These foreigners were held to be the source of much that was intolerable about crowd life in the hamlet. They were alleged to be lawless, accused of congregating in the village gin mills, and thought to be especially vulnerable to the debauching qualities of alcohol. To the "progressives" it was clear that these greenhorn aliens, with their strange ways and loyalties, could not be depended on to keep the best interests of the community in mind on Election Day.

The Democratic Party, on the other hand, found in the recent immigrants dependable, disciplined voters who were willing to cooperate for common ends. The aliens clearly had something to gain from a political principle that defended particular freedom and allowed for differences on the part of individuals. After all, both by definition and in the eyes of their neighbors, they were different. The Democrats from the back country, for their part, needed voters if they were to maintain their sway. Together the two groups found good reasons to resist improvement—the back–country people because they would have to pay for it through taxes, the immigrants because they were under constant pressure from the improvers to shape up and become like everyone else.

In dialectical terms the argument of the improvers, that is, the summation of the notions they expressed through their political activity, represents the ideological component of a forming thesis.[2] It is founded on necessities compounded out of a unique praxis—that of village existence as an enterpriser—and of the social relationships that praxis occasions. This argument also imposes certain imperatives and through their office erects antinomies. It defines "good" people and "bad," that is, acceptable people and the others; and "good"

---

2. A totalization in the terms of Jean-Paul Sartre as he uses them in *The Problem of Method,* pp. 34-84.

acts, as well, which are thesis–confirming acts. It thus excludes those who do not conform to its predilections and attaches to that exclusion certain negative connotations. The included, the anointed, the in–group of decent people are bound together by common attitudes and actions which conform to the ideal. At times when indignation runs high, leadership in an excess of zeal may demand affirmation and threaten exclusion, and as a result the in–group may become quite small. Such an approach has its disadvantages where the conventional form of action is an appeal to majority opinion. It is possible to feel very right and very certain, to seem to have all the best arguments, and still, to lose at the ballot box.

The excluded others, who have their own forms of existence to contend with, may represent different aspects of exclusion. They are less readily defined in terms of a coherent argument. In the Nyack field of action, for example, some deemed "old fogies" still held to the old Rockland ways and expressed themselves in terms straight out of the frontier. The aliens, who worked in the factories and at similar tasks, on the other hand, held to ways that had been developed on a different continent. It was their unwillingness to go along, not their agreement, that they expressed through their political opposition to improvement.

While the particular notions elaborating the improvers' argument represent new forms, their continuity with Rockland's past is also apparent. In a large measure, these notions were atavisms rooted in the frontier ways of rural Rockland and obtained much of their content and language there. Consequently, the arguments were forming, not formed, dynamic, never static. Isaac Smith and William Voorhis do not stand between a new and an old. They are both new and old, as was "Farmer" and Nicholas Gesner before him. The controversies of the forty–year period emerge out of the search for the new notions and out of the original articulation that had defined frontier existence. As a result, the argument developed in the course of these controversies was incomplete, inconsistent, and sometimes thoroughly incoherent.

Progress, as indicated earlier, was essential to the prosperity of those who supported improvement at Nyack. For the active man progress and personal success formed a unity. They involved good management and a basic optimism about the future. Success was to be achieved through God's grace and was open to any conscientious person who was willing to try, something those who dragged their feet seemed not to be able to understand. Failure, on the other hand, was the product of lax morals, insobriety, and sloth. When failure occurred it was the individual's own fault; he had failed to use the intelligence God had given him, and had not shown proper gumption. Instead, he had chosen to allow evil propensities to dominate him and had scorned success.

Progress was the sum of several successes. Progress was also the development of practical arrangements through which successes became possible and for this reason became the social corollary of personal success. As God offered success to the righteous individual, He also offered progress to the collectivity of righteous individuals, a progress which brought with it further successes. Thus the active man saw it as his duty to make the village an attractive place for business in the same sense that he saw it as his duty to keep up with the times and to improve the functioning of his enterprise. It was in this manner that improvement in the village became a moral imperative.

As had been true of the back country earlier, there was always much to be done at Nyack. Sidewalks needed building, so that the ladies in residence at the resort hotels could promenade in comfort; sewers needed digging, and delinquent elements needed correcting. Otherwise, the peace that made progress possible would be absent and right–thinking men would be found wanting.

Often, that which needed doing could be done by an individual as part of his private effort. A merchant would erect a street lamp to attract customers and at the same time to light the way of passers–by. A businessman might pay to clean out the town pump. Then there was the lady who entered the gin mill to pray for the poor souls she found congregated there, and the interested citizen who visited the schools to check on the level of instruction. The *Journal's* editor frequently took note of such "improvements" and complimented the doers for their contribution to the general good. A practical utilitarianism prevailed in the village as it had on the back–country farms; at Nyack, thanks to the newspapers, its good offices could be acknowledged.

The successful and those who aspired to success responded to the manifold tasks of village improvement with enthusiasm. The three movements recapitulated are samples drawn from their con cerned efforts as a group. The movements, themselves, however, were larger in scope than was the response that inspired them, and included expressions of the opponents as well as of the proponents of improvement.

The movements were primarily social in their impact. While they did touch on the improvement of facilities, especially in the case of village incorporation, their main thrust was towards shaping personal inclinations. Originally, the question was how to encourage the natural good in people; in time, it shifted to how to develop proper attitudes in the several minds of the heterogeneous crowd. In the early days moral suasion was often sufficient, but with the passage of time the press of the crowd increased, diversity intensified, and enculturation turned out to be more difficult. In the close proximity that had developed in the village an unreasonable attitude on the part of one constituted a danger to all. A stronger hand was required if the young, the alien, and the disruptive were to be brought up to proper standards.

It was this stronger hand that was to be provided by the supporters of improvement, not so much out of meanness or desire to dominate, but because of their concern for the development of good Americans, good Nyackers who would make the place good for business. The three movements represent, in part, the articulation of this noble effort by the improvers.

Temperance, possibly the most primitive of the three, usurped many of the functions of religion in the village. It was an unembarrassed attempt to impose control on potentially disruptive individuals. Through the benevolence of the movement unstable individuals were to be helped to defend themselves against their own tendencies to destruction. Liquor seems to have been accepted quite generally as the source of a great deal of vicious, antisocial activity. The drunkards, and those who aspired to that rank, were not evil, however; by the temperance definition they were simply weak–willed. The truly evil were those who trafficked in liquor, for they were engaged in a crime against human decency and were willing to lead others into certain disaster while seeking their own profit.

Temperance drew its most ardent supporters from among business people who were still getting established, from women, and from those of the young who conceived of themselves as well–bred; in other words, primarily from among individuals who were not entirely secure in their status. With them it was a moral impulse, consistent with the prevailing philosophy of personal initiative. An evil ignored would certainly bring eventual retribution to the community, and it was the duty of right–thinking people to extirpate that manifest evil. This was God's command. So they took up the cause of virtue. Through participation in the temperance crusade certain supporters sought to acquire the respect of their fellow citizens by means of their commitment to propriety. In pursuing this aspect of their movement they joined forces with the xenophobic Know–Nothings and linked purity to nationality. "A moral people and a moral republic" became a watchword of their cause. Excluded were foreigners and those unwilling to recognize their duty as Americans, i.e., those tolerant of booze. Thus the banner of patriotism was raised in the service of the temperance crusade.

Successful people also joined the crusade, especially during its first phase. The shoe manufacturers made up a large block on the Maine Law enforcement board. They had a practical reason for controlling liquor; they required disciplined workers for their shops and stores. Furthermore, liquor was also identified as contributing both to delinquency and to increased taxes, and they believed it to their advantage to suppress its traffic. The excesses to which the fervent advocates of temperance were addicted alienated the successful, however, so that during the later phases of the crusade their role was much diminished, and they eventually left the field to the passionate.

The schools were there to train the young, no matter whose young they might be, to be proper citizens. Their support posed a true dilemma for those ideologically committed to democracy. If democracy is to function properly it is important that its participating electors be capable of intelligent discrimination among alternatives. Those committed to democracy readily accepted this principle as they also accepted the principles of relative equality of ability and resources. The many independent homesteads of the frontier society represent the material aspect of this commitment.

Expenditures for education expand with each increase in the number of the young. These outlays come out of taxation, and, as we are aware, the power to tax is the power to destroy. Thus this expansion becomes a threat and people are reluctant to face up and pay for it. This was the nature of the dilemma in Rockland County.

Back–country men were the most concerned about the taxes, but at the same time they acknowledged the importance of education. The villagers shared both these attitudes to a degree, but were also concerned about the rapid expansion of population in their localities, and about its growing heterogeneity. Consequently, throughout the period of progress, villagers pushed constantly for the expansion and improvement of education. The back–country men and those villagers close to them in point of view opposed, but each time finally gave way.

The perfection of education was a matter of different intent however. It was undertaken largely in response to the demands imposed by the emerging industrial system. A disciplined labor force and peace on the streets were central to these demands, and the growing heterogeneity of the population, while in some ways an asset, was seen primarily as an obstacle here. Improvement in education, which to a great extent meant its professionalization, functioned to provide sanctions for the new people, and to equip them for the emerging industrial system. The implied threat in Superintendent Cook's letter of 1866, that every child was under observation, is evidence of this function. No matter how they entered, whether it was as back–country hayseeds, or as first–generation Germans or Irish, as the children of illiterates or of well–educated eighth–generation Americans, they were graduated as the products of an order–enforcing agent of society. Following the completion of their training they were best identified as Nyack–New York–Americans, more definitely peas of the same educational pod than of the different pods from which they had come.

Patriotism, in offering identification, was an important element in this processing. The schools operated to induce conformity and presumably, by this means, re–introduced into the heterogeneous population some of the social homogeneity that had been a significant element in frontier society. Consequently, the processing seemed to accord well with the old traditions of democracy. Interestingly, the immigrants, whose children were prime objects of this "do–good" impulse, took little part in the controversies the schools engendered.

With incorporation some needed things got done. A measure of autonomy from the reticent back country was achieved. Roads, sidewalks, and sewers were provided and street lights erected. A police force was established and assigned a daily round, and the orders of a board of health were obeyed—albeit indifferently at times. Thus facilities, peace, and some measure of discipline were introduced, limits were prescribed, and a public good was proclaimed in the village. But there was also an ominous element. When *Journal* editor Charlton admitted his doubts about the truth of the maxim that every person is "the best judge of matters affecting his private interests," and called for some check on people's actions, he, in effect, announced the end of an era. In the village the door that the frontier had opened was fast closing.

New needs, founded on crowd conditions and technology, demanded discipline and a responsible obedience which was not quite compatible with the old freedom. Many, of course, found it difficult to reconcile themselves to necessity and for that reason many of the improvements accompanying incorporation had been botched. But, in the long run, it was clear that the future lay with an "organization with power to act for all, to study the best interests of all, to care for and protect all."[3]

All this improving took time, and even as late as the 1890s many continued to resist the encroachments of bureaucratic authority. But slowly, as the years passed, innovations of the earlier period became accepted modes of the present, and the social system closed in on the individual. The anxiety–producing disorder and confusion of the 'fifties was displaced by an awkwardly conceived legal–rational system and many of the disruptive energies of the citizens were redirected into safe outlets. This transformation was a large part of what the people who had settled at Nyack called progress. It was never completed, however, for the frontier spirit proved strong and resilient, and there is still resistance, even to this day.

A major element contributing to the success of the improvers over the long run was their claim that they represented the authentic "American" position. Through it they widened their support in the community. In formal politics this claim was not difficult to sustain, for with the increase in population in the urban areas, the Democrats became more and more dependent on the alien–born industrial worker for their support. The argument was that the Democrats had so catered to foreigners that they no longer deserved the support of loyal Americans. To give substance to this contention, the editor of the *Journal* in 1890 cynically mourned the demise of the old Democracy with the following purported anecdote:

3. *Vide supra*, p. 163.

O'Gallagher: Good mornin' Moike; fwhat do ye think of Finnegan's chances?

Moike: 'Tis horrud now to till, Pater, 'tis thot; but gegobe we do be will reprisinted on the county and town committhies so we be. I did be spellin' 'em out in the Jimocrat. There's O'Brien and McKiernan, Orangetown; Gallagher ov Clarikstown; "Mickey" Murphey and Patrick Keenan, of Haverstraw; Johnny Royan of Ramapo; and at Sthony Pint the're all Oirish, so they be; we have a dilligation there that do make one feel proud: Frank Dunnigan, Frank Griffin, Abner Carney, foine byes, they are.

O'Gallagher: But Moike, whist! Why did they allow a man named Oakley or Gilbert on our Committhees?

Moike: Steddy, bend low, Pater, and I'll tell ye; It was to catch the Amerikin vote!

As Republicans, the improvers were certain that theirs was the authentic tradition and proud of it. They not only accused their opponents, they also proclaimed their own adherence to the ancient truths. One of their number, Clarence Lexow, eventually to become a state Senator, and who, as the son of a German immigrant, had cast his lot with the improvers, underscored this conviction when in addressing himself to the question, "Why do Irishmen Vote the Democratic Ticket?" he summarized his talk with the following:

> The churches and the schools are the nurseries of Republican Principles and the bulwark of this nation's safety. When the minister is insincere and the school teacher is a fraud they are not teaching Republican principles. . . .[4]

The implication, of course, is that the teacher who does not teach Republican principles must, by definition, be a fraud.

Always the villagers needed stirring up before they were able to take action for improvement. They had to accumulate a sense of imminent need, be charged with the spirit of the occasion, and shown what could be done. Then, following these preliminaries, they were ready to act. Frequently, thanks to the dependence on passionate commitment to the cause, the excitement generated proved excessive, the boundaries of reasonableness were overstepped, and excesses developed from which retreat was necessary.

There was also always opposition. The old and the land rich and, for different reasons, the new immigrants were not as readily moved to

4. *Rockland County Journal,* October 22, 1892.

social innovation as were their youthful, energetic neighbors. However, the protests in opposition were never as energetically articulated as was the idea of progress. Instead, the opposers depended on political technique and the control of votes in developing their resistance. In response, the supporters of improvement countered with appeals to patriotism.

For all these reasons improvement was sporadic. Authority did not close in on the Nyack community at an easy pace: it erupted, then retreated, threatened, then ebbed. It had its brisk periods and its dull periods. The idea of progress and improvement depended, for its articulation, on initiative and enthusiasm, and often it stagnated for a period in a pool of apathy. The growth of the principle by which the urban structure of society was established at Nyack was, therefore, not unlike the growth of the economic system there.

14

THE "NEW MAN" GROWS OLDER

For two centuries the American land frontier was a major conditioning agent for a large segment of her people. To some, the frontier offered an avenue of escape from the restraints imposed by entrenched authority; to others, it offered fresh land and fecundity. Opportunities abounded. Once on the frontier, however, the pioneers were thrown very much on their own resources. There were few guidelines and no one to turn to in times of crisis. To survive, the people who had ventured out on the frontier had to learn to cope with exceptional circumstances which were frequently difficult. In the course of this struggle adaptability, versatility, and initiative, traits which facilitated survival, were encouraged. Their conventional mode of action tended to be voluntaristic rather than compliant and, in emphasizing innovations designed to personal taste, atomistic. Furthermore, the institutions they constructed operated to promote voluntaristic and atomistic behavior and in that way complemented the individualism they pursued. Combined, these traits and techniques formed a unique *weltanschauung* which the pioneers passed on to their children.

Calling attention to certain phenomena he had observed while traveling about in the British colonies, de Crèvecœur suggested that an important event had taken place on the frontiers of the New World. In his opinion, special circumstances there had made possible the emergence of an entirely "new man," one freed from the obligations imposed by ancient tradition and thus free to express the natural propensities of the human being. He outlined in broad strokes his impressions of this new man, using terms roughly comparable to those above.

Over a century later, commenting on the impact of the frontier in America, Turner emphasized the extent to which the frontier environment had fastened on those who had experienced it as a unique set of personal and social characteristics. His comments were similar in substance to those of de Crèvecœur, albeit far more comprehensive in detail. Eventually, in Turner's hands, and those of his supporters and critics, the new man emerged as a total socioeconomic configuration, the frontiersman. Turner, in addition, both at the time of his first announcement and subsequently, claimed that this frontiersman had left his mark on the outlook of the entire nation.

Both Turner and de Crèvecœur had made presentations which were fundamentally, if unintentionally, dialectical, and which included an important material component. In their view people were held to have responded to a special set of objective circumstances in terms conditioned by those circumstances rather than in terms defined by a previous set of experiences. Further, their response to the special circumstances was presumed to have developed in sufficient detail to represent a unified culture pattern in and of itself. As this way of living and viewing grew elaborate and comprehensive through transmittal from neighbor to neighbor and from parent to child and *vice versa,* it became in its own terms traditional—an American way to be recognized and revered. This tradition persisted in its pure form in its native habitat for a generation or two and also interpenetrated the national will.

Turner touched only lightly on the eventual fate of the frontiersman. Fascinated with the Middle West and its people, he returned again and again to them for inspiration instead of going on and developing the long–term implications of his thesis. Speculating dialectically, however, and in abstract terms, it seems clear that the frontiersman faced two possible fates. Either he survived, intact, or he reverted and became yet another variation of mankind's commonplace experience—the experience that de Crèvecœur hoped had been transcended. These were the extremes of possibility. If he survived intact, it could only be because the frontier pattern proved functional during later phases of American experience. If, on the other hand, the frontiersman reverted and a variation of conventional society reasserted itself, then it should be apparent that contradictory elements had come into play, making frontier behavior incongruous with reality.

In seeking enlightenment on this issue we chose to examine closely a place of manageable size located in the Eastern section of the United States, and regulate our examination with an ideal–type model drawn along lines indicated by the frontier thesis. The East, having been settled first surely has had the greatest opportunity to develop away from the frontier. Such transformations as might be occasioned by objective differences and internal contradictions have had time to mature there, if anywhere on the continent. The locality chosen was Nyack, a small city on the west bank of the Hudson River in Rockland County, New York. The frontier model presented was constructed from extracts of the propositions Turner, his supporters, and even his critics offered in their many–sided attempt to describe the frontier way of life. It defined the frontier as a situation characterized by a low density of population, by spatial and social isolation, by weak traditional ties, by social homogeneity, and by voluntary association.

We began by comparing life in the back country of Rockland during its early period with ideal situations as defined by the frontier model and found that the county's land frontier, in its most formal sense, had closed by 1800. Yet much that had characterized frontier days there continued some time after that date.

During Rockland's frontier days extended family units, living a homespun life, obtained a simple subsistence from the soil. The production of goods was organized on a household basis and differentiation in economic function was not far advanced beyond provisional arrangements shaped to satisfy a few necessary neighborhood needs. Trade and communication routes were crude at best, and, so discouraged both social intercourse and production for markets. The Rockland farmers were confined by circumstances to their neighborhoods and to the society existing within these neighborhoods, and while Old World traditions had not disappeared, they lacked binding force.

It is clear from the evidence that living conditions in back–country Rockland prior to 1800 encouraged the development of frontier–type attitudes, institutions, and modes of action. Small farm freeholdings predominated and provided a favorable setting for the maintenance of independence from external authority. Where collective action was required, democratic techniques of organization were commonplace. Thus, altogether, throughout the period prior to 1800, Rocklanders exhibited much of the voluntaristic–atomistic style which, according to Turner, characterized the frontier.

Only two deviations with the original model were apparent. For one, the frontier moment in Rockland continued much longer than had been expected, and for the other, land tenure rights were not as certain and absolute as had been anticipated. Both of these deviations had operated to encourage homogeneity in the population, however, and in that sense reinforced frontierlike tendencies.

During the first quarter of the nineteenth century the county began to lose its undifferentiated rural configuration. This development began when several manufacturers located in the western extremity of the county at Ramapo joined forces with a number of the progressive farmers from the eastern sections to improve connections with the landing places along the Hudson River. In time, through their combined efforts, a system of roads and railroads traversing the county was completed. This system opened up previously isolated farm areas to trade and led to the growth of market villages along the Hudson riverfront, one of which was Nyack. In the course of this growth they expanded and improved their functions and facilities and as a result provided many opportunities for the enterprising. By mid–century these villages had developed an identity of their own, distinct from that of the back country surrounding them.

When we first encountered Nyack in our narrative we found through an examination of the activities of certain villagers, notably Tunis Smith and his nephew Isaac, evidence of the persistence of frontier modes of action in the hamlet. This conforms, of course, to what we might expect, for these men had grown up in the back country and consequently had been conditioned in a frontierlike environment. At Nyack they confronted an unstructured situation which allowed them freedom in planning and action. This experience, with its high potential for exploitation by those with the traits of the frontiersman, reinforced their original attitudes.

During the period from 1850 to 1890, however, the situation at Nyack developed trends contrary to the frontier thesis. We found, in surveying incidents drawn from that period, evidence suggesting both significant transformations in the substance of experience and a retention of frontier attitudes.

Earlier, in defining the typical frontier, individuals were described in contradictory terms. While they were reputed to be enthusiastic and outgoing, they were also held to be lacking in trust and inclined to conformity. If this assessment of the frontier personality is correct, it follows, abstractly, that anyone subject to frontier conditioning might have both these contrasting tendencies, but with a difference in emphasis. While the basically enthusiastic person might have doubts, he would be inclined to cast his lot with activity and enterprise. The suspicious person, on the other hand, might have enthusiasms but, after deliberation, would cast his lot with security and accept conformity as necessary for self–protection. Thus the enthusiastic person is basically progressive, the suspicious one basically conservative. In the back country, thanks to spatial isolation and the generally modest level of enterprise, the contradiction never amounted to much.

In the village, however, matters were different; a plethora of enthusiasts had gathered there. Those among the back–country youth who were basically activist had migrated to the village seeking ventures through which to express their capacity for enterprise. Others, less secure, remained on the back–country farms and sought to conserve what they had. In time these two groups came into conflict with each other, the progressives demanding improvements and the conservatives complaining about taxes. This is the first rip in the social fabric. It was especially exacerbated by the fact that men as they grew older tended to shift their allegiance from progress to conservatism. After years of enterprise they had acquired a financial stake to defend. Being successful with solid reputations, they frequently were effective in inhibiting the very progress which they had advocated in their youth and, as a result, contributed to the frustration and resentment welling up in the minds of the succeeding generation of young activists. Consequently, the rip became a wound in the public confidence.

With the shift in the locus of activity from the rural countryside to the village, two essential features of the frontier model were violated and with that violation further tears appeared in the social fabric. First, the density of population increased dramatically; second, the population grew more heterogeneous both in character and in function. Furthermore, the two reinforced each other.

With increase, the village population came to be compressed within a relatively compact area. The spatial isolation that had characterized the frontier gave way to crowd living, and the independence born of seclusion had to be relinquished. It became necessary to establish appropriate health measures, to organize protection against lawlessness and danger from conflagration, and to take steps towards improving facilities such as the paving of the streets and the construction of a sewage disposal system. Otherwise, the way of life that had congealed at Nyack was very difficult, and at times dangerous.

Furthermore, as population increased, the numbers to be assimilated into the existing society grew rapidly. Sometimes the newcomers came in numbers sufficiently large as to be able to resist assimilation. Hence they retained, at least in part, traditional ways alien to Rockland's frontier–induced mode of living. Ethnic and class sub–communities developed within the village community and coagulation replaced the atomization of the back country. Eventually, these sub–communities claimed for themselves the rights that previously had been assigned to the separate individuals, and enforced their claims with political action.

A concentrated population also offered a vastly larger potential market for goods and services and thereby fostered economic specialization. Differentiated occupation groups, such as merchants and carpenters, and economic class groups, such as the city–employed suburbanites and the shoe factory workers, developed. In many instances, a correspondence between ethnic group and class group was apparent. As a result social techniques for the measuring of status grew more efficient. In all these ways the old social homogeneity of the back country gave way and in its place a new society appeared replete with class and status distinctions. Simultaneously, the rents in the social fabric widened and grew more numerous.

Two further consequences of the shift to the village were an intensification of the competitive struggle and an increase in the insecurities of economic life. Earlier the society of the back country was described as a steam kettle operating at a low pressure and attention was called to the pervasiveness of uncertainty and distrust there. To some extent, everyone was a stranger and a competitor. But other circumstances prevailed there to temper the animus and help make existence tolerable—for example, the neighborhood interdependence and the assemblies.

With the move to the village pressures increased markedly, distrust thickened and began to ooze out. The many unspecialized productive units of the back country were replaced by large, single–

purpose, capital–intensive firms which to survive, engaged in intense competition. Frequently they failed. Many individuals committed themselves to a specific trade and its vicissitudes and as a result grew dependent on market conditions within that single industry. In this manner they restricted their alternatives and, when faced with a crisis in their economic life, frequently found it necessary to organize for self–protection. This they did at the expense of their neighbors with whom they dealt in business affairs. Such combinations might be open, as with the Knights of St. Crispin, or furtive, as with the Upper Nyack property owners.

Together with the expansion of market–oriented production and the increase in money usage, the Rocklanders in Nyack grew more and more dependent on business conditions exogenous to the county, and gradually lost the sense that they commanded their own fate. All these factors opened further wounds in the public confidence, doubt was intensified, and, eventually, gloom settled in. Events, it seemed, were escaping control and the cherished freedom of the past was proving abrasive. At times the frustration came to be so great that it deteriorated into discord and calumny.

In response, some set about correcting the damage. Originally, those who assumed leadership in the forming community were the products of the back country, and they undertook this new task in the same spirit that their ancestors had displayed in opening the wilderness. Later others joined them in their quest, copying the ap-proaches of the initial opinion leaders. Together, they treated im-provement as if it were a field for enterprise. Defining the situation in terms of individual responsibility, they took action independently, of their own volition. Such group activity as they engaged in was at first entirely voluntary and was designed specifically for the solution of particular problems. Through their efforts they sought to make the situation at Nyack more comfortable from their point of view, and more calculable. Certainty and discipline became desired ends, and in service to them the village leaders worked for the approval of measures designed to enforce order on the association group.

Temperance, free schools, and incorporation—the three move-ments discussed in detail earlier in this study—were examples of this generalized response by the dominant people in Nyack. Eventually, all three came to be directed towards conditioning the individuals who made up the village to accept authority. In effect, they operated to produce inertia in the membership of the social group, and when they succeeded, collective principles superseded individualism, and the old freedom based on the independence of means waned.

Most solutions to village problems were made in response to a crisis, were made *ad hoc,* and were tinged with personal identification. Large but not necessarily consistent plans, combined with personal energy and insufficient means, were a common constant of these efforts. Opposition to improvement was made of much the same cloth from which advocacy had been cut; hence the constructive social moment was always a moment of dramatic conflict. As a result all these movements are evidence that frontier–type characteristics still prevailed in Nyack throughout the period ending in 1890, just as they are evidence of the development of social patterns inherently antithetical to the frontier.

So the people who had begun with an affection for freedom ended with a respect for law and order. The people who had begun with an intention to transform the world had succeeded only too well. The material base on which the voluntaristic–atomistic society had been erected during the rural period was undermined by the progress which brought forth the village, and in its place there had emerged a new base sponsoring collective judgments. The transformation, however, was incomplete—and consequently, doubly uncomfortable.

Earlier, before visions of infinite progress had enraptured it, Nyack might have accepted its limitations and settled down as a modest entrepôt, serving its back country with a degree of efficiency while at the same time introducing into the mode of living a measure of charm and beauty. It might have sought seriously to become the "gem of the Hudson"—a phrase often used locally to describe the village because of its lovely setting. But that was not to be. For, in the course of the period of progress, an event had intervened which inflated ambition at the landing, and the place that might have become a zircon, bright and shining, waxed unhappy because it was not a diamond.

This event was the industrial revolution. It touched Nyack as it touched every place in the United States in the course of the nineteenth century. The steamboat *Orange,* the shoe factories, the specialty shops were all manifest aspects of this revolution in technique. It also had its meaning for the frontier, for the enthusiasm and activity of the frontier spirit provided the human energy that made the revolution possible. Just as it had encouraged the pioneers in making the first improvements on their homesteads and in seeking the grace of God, the frontier spirit also encouraged them to participate in undertakings clothed in the new technology. As a participant in this momentous event, Nyack was, of course, caught up in its sweep. At the same time, the revolution itself contributed to the survival of frontier attitudes.

These beliefs, however, were fertilized in a different soil from that of the old frontier. For the material imperatives of industrialism ran directly counter to the independent spirit of the back–country homestead. In the new milieu created by technology, people were fixed into roles which came to stand for them and defined their possibilities. They specialized as machinists or photographers or teachers. These roles, emergent in factories, in bureaucracies, and in dealerships, were narrowly conceived and for most implied subservience. They imposed dependence and demanded orderliness. The result was a combination of frontier euphoria and industrial discipline. The frontier attitudes persisted—were encouraged, in fact—because they helped people function effectively in their assigned roles. The belief that one could still make a fortune or, at least, could rise within the system, provided a strong incentive to work hard. Such beliefs, however, persisted primarily as illusion; for it was necessary, if the factory-society was to work. to condition individuals to accept the passive roles assigned them. They were obliged to maintain the essential enthusiasm imparted by the frontier while at the same time deluding themselves about its source. It was in this manner that the new man of de Crève-cœur grew older, and in that growing, lost his innocence.

As for the illusion that the world was still there to win, it developed an existence independent of day–to–day practical circumstances. Events no longer confined it tightly to mundane matters and only rarely confirmed it. In this form it contrasted sharply with its prior existence as the ideal component of frontier experience. Aspiration had been free to flow then because practical possibilities provided limits to the choices taken. While back–country men received continual reassurance through achievement in their endeavors and in time developed a measure of true pride, the very circumstances of their existence kept their achievements within modest limits. In that situation negative features characteristic of the frontier attitude proved to be of little consequence, and its positive features predominated.

In the villages the frontier attitudes slowly came to be transformed into illusion as they proved only partially compatible with practical circumstances. As a result the pride which had moved people earlier lost its down–to–earth quality and, as fancy, encouraged a sense of omnipotence. Given gumption, get–up–and–go, anything was presumed to be possible, and in that very personality–oriented milieu such limits as appeared came to be attributed to weakness or wickedness. These limits were never seen as situational, or due to circumstances outside human control. When a good fellow failed it was because he had not kept up with the times, or because he had used his capital unwisely. For others, failure implied that those who failed were either wicked, illiterate, or the victims of demon drink. When difficulties that were general in impact were encountered, such as in 1878, the grandsons of the frontier still sought to identify the malefactors, the individuals who had presumably brought on those troubles. As the environment was deemed to be benevolent, general difficulties could hardly stem from it. Omnipotence demanded that there be a human explanation instead.

In seeking about, pejoratively, those who assumed leadership in the community settled again and again on the very element that had been the original source of their magnificent energy—the self–interest that had brought them to the village and had set them to their tasks. Only now they spoke of it as avarice. In the back country it had been a gentle fault, one that lubricated activity. Except for the small measure of interpersonal hostility it encouraged, it was largely innocuous. But in the village avarice came to be seen as the root of all evil, as a malignancy which inspired distrust and sponsored invidious class distinctions. It infected the wounds that population pressure and heterogeneity had inflicted on the social order and kept suspicion alive. Nevertheless, the villagers continued to persist in the belief that self–interest dominated legitimate motivation and were dubious of those who claimed to speak for the general good. As a result of this conflict in beliefs, the general good proved exceedingly difficult to achieve.

The immediate consequence of this double–thinking was that no social act other than one expressed as a conglomerate of individual efforts was possible. And, since each of these individual efforts was plagued by distrust, in combination they inspired controversy rather than confidence. Consequently, the public effort of the community remained hesitant and tentative throughout.

Thus the frontier remained influential in village life, but primarily as a set of contradictory principles that were frequently at odds with reality. The frontier continued to move people to action as individuals while at the same time inhibiting their combined efforts. By 1890 in Nyack its force had diminished. It had become sporadic and uncertain in its impact, and the achievements it sponsored remained incomplete and provisional. The "new men" who had been born free to strive and had been raised charged with energy to act had given way to others who subscribed to many of the ideals of the frontier while devoting their lives to a system demanding order and submissiveness.

APPENDIX

ESTIMATED POPULATION OF THE VILLAGE OF NYACK

1800–1900
(Including the portion of the village
of Clarkstown where possible)

Year		Population
1800	Orangetown only	100+
1810	Orangetown only	200+
1820	Orangetown only	200+
1830	Orangetown only	300+
1840	Orangetown only	700+
1850	Orangetown only	1000+
1860	Orangetown and Clarkstown	2481
1870	Orangetown and Clarkstown	3650
1880	Orangetown and Clarkstown	4473
1890	Orangetown and Clarkstown	6275
1900	Orangetown and Clarkstown	6410

The years of most rapid growth are 1830–1860, 1869–1873, and 1883–1893. Growth slows almost to a halt after 1893.

The estimates are the author's and are based on the following sources: Manuscripts of Census, Federal, for Rockland County, *Rockland County Journal, City and Country,* Frank B. Green, *The History of Rockland County,* David Cole, ed., *History of Rockland County, New York,* and A. S. Tompkins, ed., *History of Rockland County.*

BIBLIOGRAPHY

ROCKLAND COUNTY MATERIALS

A History of the Classis of Paramus of the Reformed Church in America, The Board of Publication, Reformed Church in America, 1902.

An Argument Delivered on the Part of New York to settle or determine the boundary lines between the Colonies of New York and New Jersey, 8 October 1767. Delivered by J. M. Scott, James Duane, and Benj. Kissam. (Rare Book Room, New York Public Library).

Bailey, Rosalie Fellows, *Pre-Revolutionary Dutch Houses and Families,* William Morrow & Co., 1936.

Budke, George H. and J. E. Christie, *Old Nyack,* Nyack National Bank, 1928.

Budke, George H., *Budke Collection:* An extensive collection of some 90 sets of miscellaneous documents, manuscripts, maps, deeds, and other data pertaining to Rockland County. The several items are in no particular order but are numbered and can be identified at the library by a number sequence BC-1, BC-2, etc. (Manuscript Room of the New York Public Library). The museum library of the Historical Society of Rockland County has a card index of the collection based on these numbers. The items identified below in this bibliography comprise only a small part of the collection.

Budke Collection, BC-61: *Centennial Publication of the Greenbush Presbyterian Church of Blauvelt,* New York, 1912.

Budke Collection, BC-21: *Documents,* a scrapbook containing a variety of legal papers, some of which are originals.

Budke Collection, BC-34, 35, 72, 73, & 74: *Historical Manuscripts.* Vol. A-E. A collection of uncatalogued documents.

Budke Collection, BC-70, 71: *Historical Miscellanies,* vol. I and II. Typed copies of source documents collected by Mr. Budke in 1923, bound with pages unnumbered.

Budke Collection, BC-23: *Orangetown Tax List for the Year 1796,* the actual notebook kept by the collector, Abraham G. Blauvelt, that year.

Budke Collection, BC-36: *Original Records of Orangetown, 1765-1819.* The book of minutes of the town meetings for those years, handwritten.

Budke Collection, BC-29: *Papers Relating to the New York and New Jersey Boundary Controversy, 1686-1775.* Collected and compiled by Mr. Budke in 1924.

Census, Federal

    Heads of Families at the First Census of the United States Taken in the Year 1790, New York, Baltimore, Genealogical Publishing Co., 1966.

    Census Manuscripts for 1800, 1810, 1820, 1830, 1840, 1850, 1860, 1870, and 1880 (microfilm, New York Public Library).

Census, New York State

    1855—Manuscripts (Rockland County Clerk's office for Haverstraw and Ramapo only).

    1865 and 1892—Manuscripts (Clerk's office and complete for the county).

    1875—Manuscripts (Clerk's office, but not complete).

City and Country, a weekly newspaper published at Nyack, New York 1859 through 1916. The Nyack Public Library has complete file on microfilm beginning October 2, 1885 and ending September 9, 1916, plus scattered issues prior to 1885.

Christie, J. Elmer, *An Interview with L. W. Coates,* in 1914. Mr. Christie's notes from this interview are on file in the Nyack Public Library. Mr. Coates, who was born in 1825 or 1827, describes Nyack as he knew it c. 1835.

Clinton, Charles, *The Marble Covered Field Book,* BC-30. Copied by Mr. Budke in 1923 from the original in the Orange County Courthouse, Goshen, N.Y.

Cole, Rev. David, ed., *History of Rockland County, New York,* with biographical sketches of its prominent men, J. B. Beers & Co., 1884.

Cole, Rev. David, *History of the Reformed Church of Tappan, New York,* Stettiner, Lambert, & Co., 1894.

DeNoyalles, John, *Debates in Dividing Orange County, New York, A Humorous Speech in Broken English,* New York, 1774. (Rare Book Room, New York Public Library).

Ecclesiastical Records of the State of New York, vol. I to IV, James B. Lyon, publ., 1901.

French, J. H., *Historical and Statistical Gazetteer of New York State,* R. P. Smith, 1860. (Reprinted by Kennikat Press, 1969)

Gordon, Thomas F., *Gazetter of the State of New York, 1836.*

Green, Frank B., *Notes on Nyack,* a history of Nyack printed serially in the Rockland County Journal from March 2, 1878 to June 15, 1878. (Nyack Library).

Green, Frank B., *The History of Rockland County,* A. S. Barnes & Co., 1886.

Haring, John J., *Floating Chips,* 1924. Reminiscences from his youth in the Rockland back country in the 1830s and 40s.

Harvey, Cornelius B., ed., *Geneological History of Hudson and Bergen Counties,* New Jersey Geneological Publishing Company, 1900.

Hasenclever, Peter, *The Remarkable Case of Peter Hasenclever.* (Rare Book Room, New York Public Library).

Hewitt, Edward R., *Ringwood Manor, the Home of the Hewitts,* Trenton Printing Co., 1947.

Minutes of the General Meeting of School District #4, Rockland County, New York. From December 5, 1864. (Office of the District Superintendent of Schools, Nyack, N.Y.).

Minutes of the Village of Nyack, First Incorporation, From November 18, 1872 to July 20, 1875. (Office of the Village Clerk of Nyack).

Nyack Evening Journal, a daily newspaper published in Nyack, New York. Began publication May 6, 1889 as a companion paper to the weekly *Rockland County Journal.* Became the *Journal-News* on July 1, 1932. (Microfilm, Nyack Public Library).

Nyack Star, a daily newspaper published in Nyack, New York. Began publication July 27, 1892 as a companion paper to the weekly *City and Country.* (File beginning June 27, 1892 and ending December 30, 1916 Nyack Public Library.)

O'Callaghan, E. B., ed., *Documents Relative to the Colonial History of the State of New York,* vol. I to XIV. Collected by John R. Broadhead. Weed, Parsons, & Co., 1856.

O'Callaghan, E. B., ed., *The Documentary History of the State of New York,* vol. I to IV. Weed, Persons & Co., 1849.

Palisades Library Papers: The Library of Palisades, New York, has on file a number of interesting papers relating to land titles in Palisades, to the history of Sneden's Landing and of the ferry across the Hudson at that point. The most important document there is the handwritten manuscript of the *Diary* of Nicholas Gesner, beginning October 3, 1830 and continuing until 1853. These papers were collected by Wilfred Gilman sometime around 1900.

Pierson, Edward F., *The Ramapo Pass,* unpublished, in typescript. Budke Collection BC-27. 1927.

Ransom, James M., *Vanishing Ironworks of the Ramapos,* Rutgers University Press, 1966.

Rockland County Journal, a weekly newspaper published in Nyack, New York. Began publication August 3, 1850. Eventually became the daily *Rockland Journal-News.* (Complete on microfilm with the exception of the years 1881 and 1882, Nyack Public Library.)

Rockland Record, a publication of the Rockland County Society of the State of New York. Vol. I (1930), vol. II (1931-32), and vol. III (1940) were the only volumes published. This publication makes extensive use of the work of George H. Budke.

Salisbury Family Papers: Available at the museum library of the Historical Society of Rockland County, Orangeburg, N.Y. Among the papers in this collection are documents relating to the Nyack Turnpike, the steamboat *Orange,* and family records of the Smith, Kuyper, and Cornelison families. This collection includes the *Diary* of Tunis Smith.

Sickels, John E., *Notebook* and other papers. In possession of his granddaughter, Mrs. Ann Mathews of Orangeburg, N.Y.

Tompkins, Arthur S., ed., *Landmarks of the Lower Hudson Valley and History of Rockland County,* Van Deusen and Joyce, 1902.

FRONTIER THESIS AND GENERAL

Billington, Ray Allen, *America's Frontier Heritage,* Holt, Rinehart and Winston, 1966. See especially the bibliography on the frontier, pp. 285-302.

Billington, Ray Allen, ed., *The Frontier Thesis, Valid Interpretation of American History?* Holt, Rinehart, and Winston, 1966.

Bohannan, Paul & Fred Plog, eds., *Beyond the Frontier,* The Natural History Press, 1967.

Burkhart, J. A., "The Turner Thesis: A Historian's Controversy," *Wisconsin Magazine of History,* vol. 31, (1947-1948), pp. 70-83.

Cochran, Thomas C., *New York and the Confederation,* University of Pennsylvania Press, 1932.

Commager, Henry Steele, ed., *America in Perspective,* Random House, 1947.

Craven, Avery, *Democracy in American Life, A Historical View,* The University of Chicago Press, 1941.

Curti, Merle, *et al., The Making of an American Community, A Case Study of Democracy in a Frontier County,* Stanford University Press, 1959.

Curti, Merle, "The Section and the Frontier in American History: the Methodological Concepts of Frederick Jackson Turner," in *Methods in Social Science,* edited by Stuart A. Rice, Chicago, 1931.

de Crèvecœur, J. Hector St. John, *Letters from an American Farmer,* E. P. Dutton & Co., Inc., 1957.

de Tocqueville, Alexis, *Democracy in America,* trans. by George Lawrence, ed. by J. P. Mayer, Doubleday & Co., Inc., 1969.

Dunlap, William, *History of the New Netherlands Province of New York,* vol. I and II, Carter and Thorpe, 1840.

Elkins, Stanley and Eric McKitrick, "A Meaning for Turner's Frontier," *Political Science Quarterly,* vol. LXIX (1954), pp. 321-353 and 565-602.

Encyclopaedia of the Social Sciences, Macmillan Co., 1937, Vol. VI, articles on the "Frontier."

Flick, Alexander C., *Loyalism in New York During the American Revolution,* The Columbia University Press, 1901.

Fox, Dixon Ryan, ed., *Sources of Culture in the Middle West, Backgrounds versus Frontier,* D. Appleton-Century Co., 1934.

Fox, Dixon Ryan, *The Decline of Aristocracy in the Politics of New York,* Columbia University, 1919.

Hofstadter, Richard and Seymour Martin Lipset, eds., *Turner and the Sociology of the Frontier,* Basic Books, 1968.

Hofstadter, Richard, "Turner and the Frontier Myth," *The American Scholar,* vol. 18 (1949), pp. 433-443.

Horner, Harlan Hoyt, ed., *Education in New York State 1784-1954,* The University of the State of New York, 1954.

Kane, Murray, "Some Considerations on the Safety Valve Doctrine," *The Mississippi Valley Historical Review, vol. XIII* (1936), pp. 169-188.

Laing, R. D., and D. G. Cooper, *Reason and Violence,* Tavistock Publications, 1964.

Mark, Irving, *Agrarian Conflicts in Colonial New York, 1711-1775,* Columbia University Press, 1940. (Reprinted by Kennikat Press, 1964.)

Paxson, Frederic L., *History of the American Frontier, 1763-1893,* Houghton Mifflin Co., 1924.

Paxson, Frederic L., *The Great Demobilization and other Essays,* University of Wisconsin Press, 1941.

Paxson, Frederic L., *When the West is Gone,* Henry Holt and Co., 1930.

Pierson, George W., "The Frontier and American Institutions," *The New England Quarterly,* vol. XV (1942), pp. 224-255.

Potter, David M., *People of Plenty: Economic Abundance and the American Character,* The University of Chicago Press, 1954.

Reich, Jerome R., *Leisler's Rebellion, A Study of Democracy in New York, 1664-1720,* The University of Chicago Press, 1953.

Sartre, Jean–Paul, *The Problem of Method,* trans. by Hazel E. Barnes, Methuen & Co., Ltd., 1963.

Schutz, Alfred, "The Social World and the Theory of Social Action," *Social Research,* vol. XXVII (1960), pp. 203-221.

Smith, William, *History of New York,* Ryer Schermerhorn, 1814.

Sweet, W. W., *Religion in the Development of American Culture, 1765-1840,* Charles Scribner's Sons, 1952.

Turner, Frederick Jackson, *The Frontier in American History,* Henry Holt and Co., 1920.

Vidich, Arthur J. and Joseph Bensman, *Small Town in Mass Society,* Princeton University Press, 1968.

Vogt, Evon Z., *Modern Homesteaders, The Life of a Twentieth–Century Frontier Community,* The Belknap Press of Harvard University Press, 1955.

Wabeke, B. H., *Dutch Emigration to North America, 1624-1860,* The Netherlands Information Bureau, 1944.

Williams, William Appleman, *The Roots of the Modern American Empire,* Random House, Inc., 1969.

INDEX